JEWISH PHILOSOPHY A–Z

Forthcoming Volumes in the Philosophy A–Z Series

Jewish Philosophy A–Z

Aaron W. Hughes

Edinburgh University Press

© Aaron W. Hughes, 2005

Edinburgh University Press Ltd
22 George Square, Edinburgh

Typeset in 10.5/13 Sabon
by TechBooks India, and printed and
bound in Finland by WS Bookwell

A CIP record for this book is
available from the British Library

ISBN 0 7486 2218 7 (hardback)
ISBN 0 7486 2177 6 (paperback)

The right of Aaron W. Hughes
to be identified as author of this work
has been asserted in accordance with
the Copyright, Designs and Patents Act 1988.

Contents

Contents

Series Editor's Preface

Religious philosophy has always been something of an enigma. In so far as it is philosophy how can it be religious, and in so far as it is religious how can it be philosophical? Our series is not the place to resolve these issues, but Aaron W. Hughes' book does bring out the interest for philosophers in Jewish philosophy. This potential conflict between reason and religion was deeply felt by many Jewish thinkers, and it gave their work an apologetic flavour, as though they had to justify what they were doing to both the religious and the philosophical communities. But of course these are very modern distinctions and at the time during which many of these thinkers were working the intellectuals in the community were expected to encompass a variety of disciplines, and they certainly did. So they brought to their philosophical analysis a deep relationship with Judaism, and this gives their work an interesting orientation. This is an area of philosophy where terminology is often difficult to understand since it is unfamiliar, and this book is designed to make access to Jewish philosophy easier. Those familiar with philosophy will find useful explanations of the religious terminology, while those acquainted with Judaism will become aware of how it can be applied to philosophical issues. In fact, it is a mistake to separate religions from philosophy, since as religions develop over time philosophical issues become very much part and parcel of the religious discourse itself, and so inseperable from the religion. With its description of leading thinkers and concepts in Jewish philosophy this book illustrates that nicely.

Oliver Leaman

Introduction

What is 'Jewish Philosophy'? At first glance, this term might seem easy to define. Jewish philosophy is simply philosophy done by Jews. Although on one level this is certainly correct, such a definition still leaves undefined two crucial terms: 'Jews' and 'philosophy'. The term 'Jew' (or 'Jewish' or 'Judaism') implies a commitment to a particular set of texts and a specific way of life. As far as texts are concerned, the central written record of the Jewish religious tradition is found in the Hebrew Bible (as opposed to the Old Testament) and other literature associated with the rabbis (e.g. midrash, Talmud). Moreover, the specific 'way of life' is one that revolves around the centrality of Jewish peoplehood and one that is sanctified by the knowledge and observance (realising that there are a number of different degrees of observance) of the divine commandments. Any form of 'Jewish philosophy', therefore, is going to have to take seriously these two trajectories.

Philosophy, in contrast, is both similar and dissimilar to Judaism. It is similar in that it also implies a commitment to a particular way of life and, therefore, is based on a specific orientation to the world. However, it is dissimilar in that this orientation is based neither on revelation nor on the particularity of a specific group of people. Rather, philosophy is usually regarded as synonymous with the rational investigation of the universe based on well-established logical and scientific principles.

Once we join together the particularism that is associated with the adjective 'Jewish' and the universalism inherent to the noun 'philosophy', we would seem to be left with some sort of oxymoron. This perplexity is compounded by the fact that virtually none of the individuals to whom we refer as 'Jewish philosophers' would have used this term to designate themselves. Philo (c. 15 BCE–c. 50 CE), for example, was born a Jew and lived a Jewish life, but when he wrote philosophy he did not consciously write something we would today recognise as 'Jewish philosophy'. Rather, he read the particular texts of Judaism in light of the universal truth claims supplied by the philosophical system of his day (i.e. that of Plato and Aristotle). Based on this, he sought to connect the Bible to these broader claims, for what was true in Judaism's sacred scripture had to adhere to what other sources of knowledge deemed true. The same could be said for virtually all of the Jewish philosophers from Philo until the nineteenth century. Thus, thinkers as diverse as Maimonides, Crescas, Mendelssohn and Krochmal – all of whom are today regarded as canonical in a discipline known as 'Jewish philosophy' – did not perceive themselves to be 'Jewish philosophers' engaged in the practice of writing 'Jewish philosophy'.

Yet, even though such thinkers did not regard themselves to be Jewish philosophers, they are today referred to by this term. So, whether they would have liked it or not, we must attempt to define 'Jewish philosophy'. To venture a definition, I would have to say something like *Jewish philosophy is the reading of the authoritative sources of Judaism (esp. the Bible) in light of the vocabulary and categories imported from philosophy.* So although the particular datum of Jewish philosophy, namely, the Bible, has not changed, the particular form of philosophy used to interpret it has. Since philosophy is not a Jewish invention, but tended to be imported from the larger cultural contexts in which Jews lived, the particular philosophical systems used to elucidate Judaism and Jewish sources were (and still are) dependent upon larger intellectual currents found in various temporal, spatial and geographic contexts.

Historically, Jews lived in diverse areas, many of which were important centres of philosophy. In antiquity this included Rome and Alexandria; in the medieval period these centres included Spain, Provence and the Eastern Islamic world; the Renaissance witnessed a sizeable community in Italy; and in the modern period Jews have lived and continue to live in places such as Germany, France and North America. In all of these diverse times and places Jews adopted and adapted to meet their own needs the philosophical schools of, for example, Platonism, Aristotelianism, Neoplatonism, Humanism, Idealism, Existentialism and Post-Modernism. Moreover, a glance at these diverse geographic and temporal locations, not to mention the various philosophical schools associated with them, reveals that Jewish philosophers served as important conduits between non-Jewish and Jewish cultures.

In order to test the above definition of Jewish philosophy, let us compare Bob Dylan, Augustine and Maimonides. Is Bob Dylan a Jewish philosopher? On the one hand, he is Jewish by birth and, for parts of his career at least, he has identified with being Jewish. Moreover a song such as 'The Times They Are A Changin'' is obviously part of a larger cultural movement of protest and civic disobedience associated with the United States in the 1960s. On the other hand, just because Dylan is a Jew and composes lyrics influenced by the broader *Zeitgeist* does not automatically make him a 'Jewish philosopher'. Why? Because he does not interpret traditional Jewish sources, nor do his lyrics have any real interest in or sustained engagement with the biblical narrative.

Unlike Dylan, Augustine (354–430 CE) was not born Jewish, yet he has a real interest in the Bible, which he interprets in light of the philosophical culture of late antiquity. Does this make him a 'Jewish philosopher'? No, because Augustine interprets the Old Testament as opposed to the Hebrew Bible. (The Old

Testament includes all of the same books as the Hebrew Bible, but arranges them in a different order and interprets them in the light of the 'New' Testament.) As a result Augustine interprets the Bible in ways (e.g. the figure of Jesus and the new covenant) that would be completely foreign to a Jewish reading of the Hebrew Bible.

Maimonides (1138–1204), however, would fit our criteria for being a 'Jewish philosopher'. He was born Jewish, lived an observant Jewish life, and interpreted the Bible (in addition to rabbinic literature) according to the broader claims of medieval Aristotelianism. Like those Jewish philosophers before and after him, Maimonides was engaged in a project of translating the vocabulary, themes and categories of the Hebrew Bible into the rationalist discourse that philosophy provided.

Although they would often come under severe criticism for reading the universal and scientific terms of the day into Judaism, those who engaged in Jewish philosophy did not see it this way at all. For them, it was, and indeed still is, a religious obligation to engage in philosophy. The scientific investigation of the world is tantamount to knowledge of God, which Jewish philosophy through its many diverse incarnations has equated and, for the most part, continues to equate with the love of God.

Acknowledgements

I would like to thank Oliver Leaman for encouraging me to write this little volume. He read over the manuscript, making various suggestions and emendations, on numerous occasions. I would also like to acknowledge Daniel Rynhold, Shai Cherry and Lisa A. Hughes for reading and commenting on various drafts of what would eventually become the present volume. I take full responsibility for all remaining mistakes and lacunae.

When writing this book I had a particular audience in mind. The day that Oliver asked me if I was interested in writing this book was, coincidentally, the same day that my wife informed me of the impending arrival of our first child. Rebecca Sophia has accordingly been involved in every part of this project. Since my goal was to present Jewish philosophy to someone who had very little familiarity with the topic, I began to conceive of her as this theoretical 'someone'. May she grow up to the delights of the Jewish tradition, including its strong commitment to matters of the intellect.

Using This Book

This proved to be a very difficult and, at times frustrating, book to write. Although obviously I think a brief introduction to the major individuals, terms and themes of Jewish philosophy is necessary, the distillation of a thinker's *oeuvre* or the mapping of a term's often diverse use over a thousand years is an impossible task. In order to negotiate the brevity of the entries, I have tried a number of different approaches to facilitate broader discussions that are meant to run through a number of entries. For example, under 'creation' I have put a number of terms (creation; creation a parte ante; creation a parte post; creation, eternal) in order to (1) convey the centrality of the problem creation poses for Jewish philosophy, and (2) to provide a larger discussion of this topic than only the one entry would afford. In other places I make a somewhat artificial distinction between medieval and modern Jewish philosophy in the service of space. For example, under 'prophecy' I primarily focus on the medieval discussion, whereas under 'revelation' I examine the modern discussion. Furthermore, I have found it useful to include some non-Jewish thinkers (e.g. Mutazilites, Alfarabi, Heidegger) for further contextualisation. Within this context, it is necessary to remember that Jewish philosophy does not exist in a vacuum, but always develops in counterpoint to larger cultural and intellectual trends.

As I envisage it, this volume has three purposes, in ascending order of importance. The first is that of an alphabetical glossary, which will be of use to the general reader wanting to look up a particular term or individual that she finds in another work, either primary or secondary. This volume will, I trust, be helpful because, in a relatively short space, such a reader will see the breadth of the term in question, including the various ways it has been employed in the Jewish philosophical tradition.

Secondly, this volume works as an introduction to Jewish philosophy. The intricate set of cross-references following each entry is meant to reveal the internal consistency of Jewish philosophy. For example, under Maimonides there exists a set of related entries – for example, Abravanel, Isaac; Ibn Daud, Abraham; Maimonidean controversies; Spinoza, Baruch – that are meant to give a much broader overview of Maimonides than only the one entry would provide. From this example, one can see that the related entries refer to Maimonides' predecessors, his successors and the broader cultural context of the role and place of Maimonides in Jewish civilisation. At the same time, however, I try not to make every term either lead to or depart from Maimonides. Ibn Daud, for example, is an important precursor of Maimonides, but he is also much more than this: he is an important philosopher in his own right, not to mention one who never would have heard of Maimonides. My entry tries to convey both perspectives; thus, it is part historical and part philosophical.

Finally, and in my opinion the most important task of this volume, is to entice readers into discovering for themselves the breadth, dynamics and beauty of Jewish philosophy. Jewish philosophy is extremely creative in its treatment of Jewish texts, and this creativity is what enabled and continues to enable Jewish philosophers to manoeuvre around the differences between Jewish and non-Jewish cultures. In so doing, Jewish philosophy is one of many processes that has led to Judaism's continuing vitality.

Before ending, I would like to supply a caveat to all that follows. No book, whether this one or any other, can ever be a substitute for reading the original sources (either in the original or in translation) of Jewish philosophy. In all of the entries devoted to individuals, I give the names (in both English translation and the original Hebrew or Arabic or German) of that individual's main works. This will, I hope, encourage the interested reader to find them at her local library. Many of these texts are not easy to read; however, I would encourage the reader to persevere and talk through some of the difficult issues with other interested readers. (The reading of both philosophy and Jewish texts is ideally a group activity.) If a reader picks up an original work of Jewish philosophy to read, this little volume will have achieved its purpose.

Jewish Philosophy A–Z

Abner of Burgos (d. 1346) was born in Spain and subsequently converted to Christianity in c. 1320 whereupon he took the name Alfonso de Valladolid. He justified his conversion on philosophical grounds in a treatise called *Offering of Jealousy* (*Minhat Kenaot*) that he sent to his former friend, **Isaac Polleqar**. The subsequent correspondence between the two is significant because it raised the polemics between Jews and Christians to a philosophical, as opposed to just an apologetic, level. Whereas many Jewish intellectuals insisted on the rationality of Judaism in order to prove its spiritual superiority over Christianity, Abner charged that Jews who remained Jewish did so only out of habituation and obduracy. In so doing, Abner was highly critical of the notion of **free will**, and he justified his conversion to Christianity based on predetermined forces. Abner's attacks on free will led to this topic becoming one of the central philosophical problems in the fourteenth century. This was also, in part, the result of the increased emphasis that certain thinkers put on **astrology**. Siding with the theologians, Abner argued for an absolute determinism that still made room for will. In the aforementioned treatise, he claimed that human actions are voluntary in so far as they are the product of will, but strictly determined in that they are part of a causal chain going back to the motion of the celestial spheres. Abner's discussion of the relationship between intellect and will, **determinism** and choice, would have a tremendous impact on subsequent philosophers (e.g. **Hasdai Crescas**).

See **apologetics; Aristotelianism; astrology; belief, celestial spheres; conversion; Crescas, Hasdai; determinism; free will; Maimonidean controversies; Narboni, Moses; Polleqar, Isaac**

Further reading: Frank and Leaman 1997

Abravanel, Isaac (1437–1508) was an important courtier, financier, biblical exegete and critic of Maimonidean rationalism. Born in Lisbon, he was forced to flee to Spain, where he became the financial advisor to King Ferdinand and Queen Isabella. His lofty position, however, did not dissuade them from issuing their infamous decree that effectively expelled the Jews from the Iberian Peninsula in 1492. Unwilling to convert to Christianity, Isaac fled to Italy where after numerous travels he died in Venice. He was well versed in the traditional sources of Judaism, in addition to the medieval Islamic and Jewish philosophical sources; he was also one of the first Jewish thinkers to cite frequently the work of both ancient Latin authors and medieval Christian theologians. Despite this there is a conservative streak that runs throughout Isaac's work.

In 1494 he wrote his *Principles of Faith* (*Rosh Amanah*), a work that, despite defending **Maimonides'** thirteen principles from attacks by **Hasdai Crescas** and **Joseph Albo**, concludes with the statement that every word of Torah is a principle that ought to be believed. The thought of Maimonides, especially his *Guide of the Perplexed*, looms largely in Isaac's work: he wrote a commentary to the *Guide*, and his *New Heavens* (*Shamayim Hadashim*) is a treatise that defends **creation** *ex nihilo* and is in direct conversation with *Guide* 2: 19.

Abravanel's most sustained work of philosophy, *The Works of God* (*Mif'alot Elohim*), is actually a critique of philosophy, providing detailed criticisms of Maimonides and other Jewish Aristotelians on issues that were of central importance to the Jewish tradition. For example, Abravanel argues that God could choose any individual to be a prophet, not just those possessing perfected intellectual faculties as implied by Maimonides. Isaac is particularly critical of Maimonides' and **Gersonides'** accounts of **miracles**, which tend to downplay their supernatural qualities in order to preserve both the order of **nature** and divine immutability. Abravanel claims, on the contrary, that miracles are supernatural events performed directly by God as the Creator of the universe.

See **afterlife; Albo, Joseph; Alghazali; Aristotelianism; belief; creation; Crescas, Hasdai; dogma; Gersonides; God, love of; God, nature of; immortality; Maimonidean controversies; Maimonides, Moses; miracles; prophecy; revelation**

Further reading: Feldman 2003; Kellner 1986; Lawee 2001; Reines 1970

Abravanel, Judah (c. 1465–after 1521), also known as Leone Ebreo, was the son of **Isaac Abravanel** and an important physician in the Spanish and later Italian courts, wrote only one surviving philosophical treatise, *The Dialogues of Love* (*Dialoghi d'amore*). This work, most likely written in Italian but not published until after his death, became a Renaissance best-seller and was translated into numerous European vernaculars. The treatise is a dialogue between Philo and Sophia on the nature of love as a sensual and cosmic principle. Heavily influenced by the Renaissance thought of **Marsilio Ficino** and **Giovanni Pico della Mirandola,** this work is somewhat paradoxical: on the one hand, it seems to have been one of the first works of philosophy written by a Jew for both a Jewish and a non-Jewish audience; yet, on the other hand, one can also read this treatise as a Jewish response to the overtly christianising agendas of Ficino and Pico.

Three major philosophical themes run throughout the *Dialogues.* First, Judah frequently provides lengthy analyses of Greek myths showing how they function as allegories that, when properly understood, are in harmony with the thought of **Moses** (indeed, he intimates that the Greeks actually stole their ideas from the Jews). Second, like **Maimonides,** Judah argues that the most authentic love is one whose object is the intellect. This is realised most fully in the intellectual vision of God. Third, Judah claims that love is what sustains and governs the entire universe, allowing the material, intellectual and divine worlds to interact with one another. Judah describes this using the image of the 'circle of love': since everything that is higher loves and desires the perfection of everything that is below it, the first half of this circle descends from God to first matter; since that which is lower desires to attain the level of that which is above, the second half of the circle ascends from first matter back up to God. Although the *Dialogues* were at first criticised by Jewish thinkers for revealing the secrets of philosophy to a general audience, they immediately became very popular among non-Jews. Eventually, however, they found a Jewish audience.

See **aesthetics; apologetics; Genesis; gentiles; God, knowledge of; God, love of; God, nature of; happiness; intellect; Maimonides, Moses; Messer Leon, David ben Judah; Messer Leon, Judah; nature; pantheism; parables; Spinoza, Baruch; Torah**

Further reading: Feldman 2003; Goodman 1992; Hughes 2004b

Abulafia, Abraham (1240–after 1291) was born in Spain, travelled widely, and was eventually condemned to death by Pope Martin IV for proclaiming the imminent arrival of the messiah (although he was subsequently spared execution owing to the Pope's own death). Author of many works, Abulafia is perhaps best known for his notion of **prophecy**. Influenced by Aristotelian philosophers, especially **Maimonides**, Abulafia argues that prophecy consists of the emanation from the **Active Intellect** into the **intellect** and **imagination** of the prophet. But, whereas Maimonides had claimed that the potential prophet must study all of the mathematical, natural and divine sciences (e.g. **metaphysics**), Abulafia contends that human perfection comes about by meditating on, reciting and manipulating the letters of the Hebrew alphabet, particularly those of the divine Name (YHWH). This theory of letter mysticism would exert considerable influence on later kabbalists (esp. in sixteenth-century Safed), in addition to those who would try to fuse together kabbalistic and philosophical teachings in the Renaissance (e.g. **Yohanan Alemanno**).

See **Abravanel, Judah; Alemanno, Yohanan; Aristotelianism; Ficino, Marsilio; God, knowledge of; God, nature of; Hebrew; imagination; intellect; kabbalah; Maimonides, Moses; Pico della Mirandola, Giovanni; prophecy; Torah**

Further reading: Idel 1989

Active Intellect: The Active Intellect (also referred to as the 'agent intellect') is a central component in medieval **cosmology**. It is the tenth and last of the celestial intellects that emanates from God, who is often equated with the first **intellect**. The Active Intellect is associated with the sphere of the moon and is regarded as the noetic mechanism responsible for the production of knowledge of the species of things in the human intellect once the latter has attained the level of acquired intellect. The Active Intellect, thus, is a supermundane agent that imparts to the human intellect the ability or power to actualise its cognitions.

Many philosophers stress the role of the Active Intellect in their theories of prophecy. For **Maimonides**, prophecy is an emanation from God through the medium of the Active Intellect into (1) the prophet's intellect and subsequently into (2) his imagination. Jewish Aristotelians also equate human **happiness** or felicity with the union (*devequt*) between the human intellect and the Active Intellect.

See **Alexander of Aphrodisias; angels; astronomy; celestial spheres; cosmology; emanation; epistemology; Halevi, Judah; happiness; imagination; immortality; intellect; Maimonides, Moses; metaphysics; Neoplatonism; Plotinus; prophecy; soul; Themistius**

aesthetics: The role of aesthetics, philosophical speculation about beauty, has always had a problematic place in Jewish thought owing to the prohibition archived in the second commandment ('You will not make for yourself any sculptured image...'). When medieval Jewish philosophers speculate about aesthetics, they do so in purely functional terms. Beauty is regarded as one of the defining characteristics of the intelligible world; objects in our world, the world of **form** and **matter**, are considered beautiful only in so far as they participate in this intelligible beauty. Yet, because physical beauty is both subject to decay and can arouse the passions (associated with the body as opposed to the soul), it is often treated with suspicion. The first full-scale attempt to create an aesthetics of Judaism may be found in **Judah Abravanel**'s *Dialogues of Love*, which discusses the interpenetration of physical and metaphysical beauty.

Modern Jewish philosophers, under the influence of **Kant**, argue that Judaism is primarily an aniconic religion that is defined by its spiritual and ethical dimensions (e.g. **Hermann Cohen**). When modern Jewish philosophers do speculate about aesthetics they tend to emphasise the poetic at the expense of the visual (e.g. **Franz Rosenzweig**). Aesthetics would play a large role in the transformation of modern Judaism as reformers sought to bring about changes in the tradition based on what they considered to be more aesthetically pleasing forms of worship (e.g. musical instruments, sermons in the vernacular).

See **Abravanel, Judah; corporeality; Enlightenment; Geiger, Abraham; Hirsch, Samson Raphael; imagination; matter; metaphysics; nature**

Further reading: Batnitzky 2000; Bland 2000; Gordon 2003; Hughes 2004a

afterlife: As with so many of the central tenets of Judaism, Jewish philosophers tend to interpret traditional beliefs in the light of philosophical principles. Whereas Jewish theology, for the most part, emphasises the bodily resurrection of the dead upon which judgement can be meted, philosophers tend to equate the afterlife with a disembodied state that affected only what they considered the true essence of humans (i.e. the **intellect**). Since Plato stressed the immortality of the soul, and Aristotle claimed that the soul was the form of a living body, Jewish philosophers primarily focus their speculation on the soul (in which was located the intellect) as the locus of **immortality** and, thus, the afterlife. Some follow **Avicenna** in arguing that individual souls retain their individuality in the world of the intellect; others follow **Averroes** who claimed that the fully actualised immortal human intellect merges into the **Active Intellect**, thereby losing all traces of individuality. Despite this rather important difference, most philosophers agree that the afterlife is reserved for only those who have perfected their intellects through the study of the philosophical sciences, thus making little or no room for average Jews who did not study. Other thinkers – such as **Saadia Gaon**, and the more conservative **Judah Halevi** and **Isaac Abravanel** – argue that the afterlife is not just reserved for the soul, but involves the physical resurrection of the body.

Modern Jewish philosophers tend not to speculate about the afterlife as much as their medieval colleagues did. And, when they do, it tends to be more generic. For example, **Franz Rosenzweig** argues that humans must constantly strive to be like God thus redeeming him and the world. The afterlife now becomes trans-personal or universal as opposed to something that involves particular individuals, thereby becoming more of an ahistorical process than a particular event in the life of an individual.

See **Abravanel, Isaac**; **Active Intellect**; **Alexander of Aphrodisias**; **Aristotelianism**; **corporeality**; **dogma**; **epistemology**; **halakhah**; **Halevi, Judah**; **happiness**; **immortality**; **intellect**; **Maimonidean controversies**; **Maimonides, Moses**; **Messianic Era**; **Neoplatonism**; **Platonism**; **Plotinus**; **religious language**; **Rosenzweig, Franz**; **Saadia Gaon**; **soul**

Albalag, Isaac (d. c. 1300), born in Provence or Catalonia, was a radical Aristotelian, who translated **Alghazali**'s *Intentions of the Philosophers* into Hebrew (and which was subsequently commented on by **Isaac Polleqar**) essentially as a pretext for expounding the scientific system of **Averroes**. Albalag's only work of philosophy is entitled *The*

Righting of Doctrines (*Tikkun ha-De'ot*), which includes a **commentary** on the account of **creation** in the book of **Genesis**. Although *The Righting of Doctrines* functions as a commentary to the aforementioned work of Alghazali, Albalag is generally quite critical not only of Alghazali but also of what he perceived to be the theological conservativism of **Maimonides**. Although the tenor of the work as a whole is critical of Alghazali, Albalag nonetheless claims that there were certain doctrines (e.g. immortality of the **soul**, God's rewarding the just and punishing the wicked) that were politically expedient and therefore the masses must be taught to believe in them. Philosophy, in contrast, is only for the intellectual elite and must not be taught to the ignorant. Albalag is usually considered to hold a version of the 'double-truth' theory that was popular among many Averroists: when faith and philosophy collide, both have to be accepted as true but in different ways (i.e. he does not try to reconcile them in the way that Maimonides did). An example of this concerns the **creation** of the world, by which Albalag contends that the world is eternally created by God as the First Cause. In so doing, he criticises Maimonides for claiming that Aristotle was uncertain that the world was eternal.

See **Alghazali; Aristotelianism; Averroes; commentary; cosmology; creation; creation, eternal; Ibn Kaspi, Joseph; Maimonides, Moses; Narboni, Moses; parables; Polleqar, Isaac; religion; religious language; soul; Torah**
Further reading: Frank and Leaman 1997; Sirat 1985

Albo, Joseph (1380–1444), a disciple of **Hasdai Crescas**, is most famous for his *Book of Principles* (*Sefer ha-Ikkarim*). The impetus behind the composition of this work is his official attendance at the disputation of Tortosa (Spain) in 1413–14. The Church inaugurated such disputations and in them Jewish delegates would have to meet various charges levelled against them by Christians (often knowledgeable, apostate Jews), the goal being that the Jews in attendance would see the errors of their ways and convert to Christianity. Albo composed this treatise to elucidate the principles of Judaism that would serve as the foundation of the tradition. His purported goal is to study all human laws, for only within this context is a definition of divine law possible. Although there are many candidates for the title divine law, Albo contends that only the **Torah** truly fits all of the criteria that he has established.

Albo claims that the law has a political purpose: to guide humans towards true **happiness**. He begins his treatise citing Aristotle and the importance of philosophical knowledge and proper conduct for human happiness; however, Albo argues that the unaided human intellect cannot determine which views are true and which are false without divine guidance. Much of the rest of the book explains, to use Albo's own words, 'those principles which pertain to a divine law generally, principles without which a divine law cannot be conceived'. For Albo, a divine law consists of three basic principles: (1) the existence of God, (2) Torah from Heaven, and (3) retribution. Albo reasons that without belief in God we cannot believe in the Torah from heaven; without belief in these two principles, we cannot believe in divine retribution. Although Albo eventually subdivides these fundamental principles into derivative principles (e.g. Mosaic prophecy) and obligatory beliefs (e.g. **creation** *ex nihilo*), his intent is to determine the legal status of the Jew in relation to both God and the community. Acceptance (or not) of the three basic principles, and all their subsequent elaborations, determines who is (or is not) a believer.

See **Abravanel, Isaac**; apologetics; belief; **Crescas, Hasdai**; dogma; happiness; Jewish people; **Maimonides, Moses**; **Narboni, Moses**; political philosophy
Further reading: Kellner 1986; Kreisel 2001; Rauschenbach 2002

Alemanno, Yohanan (c. 1435–after 1504) played an important role in the revival of kabbalistic studies in Italy, in the rise of Christian kabbalah (he was a teacher of **Pico della Mirandola**) and in the development of the synergy between Jewish philosophy and **kabbalah**. Although trained in the Aristotelian tradition by **Judah Messer Leon**, from whom he received a doctorate in medicine, Alemanno combines the theoretical account of nature with a more experiential or magical attempt to manipulate nature. He is thus interested in alchemy, **astrology**, **astronomy**, talismanic magic, dream interpretation and physiognomy (interpretation of a person's facial features) – all sciences that he derives from Hermetic, kabbalistic and Neoplatonic sources. Alemanno develops an organic view of nature, where various animate and inanimate bodies influence one another through sympathies and antipathies. Because of this intimate relationship between the animate and the inanimate, spiritual energy easily manifests itself in physical forms. Alemanno is also fond of the writings of **Abraham Abulafia**, and he argues that **Hebrew** was a language of mystical properties and that the mastery of nature and ultimately union with God could be achieved by the manipulation of language. Alemanno's syncretism and idiosyncratic philosophical ideas can be found in works such as *The Desire of Solomon* (*Hesheq Shlomo*) and *The Immortal* (*Hay ha-Olamim*).

See **Abravanel, Judah**; **Abulafia, Abraham**; astrology; astronomy; **Ficino, Marsilio**; God, knowledge of; God, nature of; happiness; kabbalah; Messer Leon, David ben Judah; Messer Leon, Judah; nature; Neoplatonism; pantheism; Pico della Mirandola, Giovanni; prophecy; Torah

Further reading: Hughes 2004b; Tirosh-Rothschild 1991

Alexander of Aphrodisias (fl. 205 CE) wrote commentaries on the works of Aristotle and was an important conduit in the transmission of ideas from the Greek world to the Arabo-Judaic world. Alexander provided both the vocabulary and the general framework with which to understand Aristotle's obscure discussion of intellectual cognition in the third book of his *De anima*. Alexander called the passive factor in human thinking the 'material intellect' because it could, like matter, receive various forms. What was responsible for making human intellects active was the **Active Intellect**, which for Alexander was an incorporeal, eternal substance. The human **intellect**, then, is nothing more than the disposition to cognise and, through intellection, it becomes active. Because of its materiality and its dispositional character, however, the human intellect is perishable. As such, Alexander's account leaves no room for personal **immortality**. Alexander's account did not go unchallenged, however; **Themistius** argued that the human intellect is not a disposition but a substance or form that has independent existence and is thus ungenerated and imperishable. Alexander's and Themistius' interpretations served as the two competing accounts of cognition in the medieval philosophical world.

See **Active Intellect; afterlife; Aristotelianism; emanation; epistemology; God, nature of; happiness; Ibn Bajja; immortality; intellect; matter; Neoplatonism; prophecy; Themistius; Theology of Aristotle**

Alfarabi (870–950) was the first truly systematic Islamic philosopher and an important political thinker who would exert a tremendous influence on medieval Jewish philosophy. On the whole, his system represents the creative mixture of Platonic **political philosophy** and Plotinian **metaphysics**. Among other things, he wrote a now-lost commentary to Aristotle's *Nichomachean Ethics*, in which, according to **ibn Tufayl**, he argued that human felicity is confined solely to the political (as opposed to the metaphysical) realm.

In his *Opinions of the Citizens of the Virtuous State* (*Mabādi ārā ahl al-madina al-fādila*), Alfarabi posits that humans are political animals and that their **happiness** is best attained in a virtuous city, which is characterised by the perfection of its laws as set forth by a prophet-philosopher-statesman. In *The Attainment of Happiness* (*Tahsīl al-sa'āda*), a text that combines Plato's political theory with Aristotle's ethics, he is primarily concerned with harmonising philosophy and **religion**. Both religion and philosophy comprise the same subjects and both give an account of the ultimate principles of being. In particular, religion is an imitation of, and thus inferior to, philosophy; whereas the latter is based on demonstration and meant for the intellectual elites, the former is based on persuasion and **imagination** in order to appeal to the masses. A corporeal afterlife, as depicted in the Koran, for example, is not an accurate account of human immortality but reflects the accommodation of the prophet to the uneducated.

Crucial to Alfarabi's system is his prophetology: the prophet, as the perfect philosopher, possesses both the theoretical sciences, in order to discover and contemplate truth, and a perfect imaginative faculty for explaining them to others. This prophetology would exert considerable influence on Jewish philosophers, most notably

Maimonides. Other important works of Alfarabi's include his various commentaries on the writings of Aristotle, *The Enumeration of the Sciences* (*Ihsā al-ulūm*), *The Treatise concerning the Intellect* (*Risāla fī al-aql*) and *The Political Regime* (*al-Siyāsa al-madaniyya*).

See **Active Intellect; afterlife; commentary; ethics; happiness; logic; Maimonides, Moses; metaphysics; political philosophy; prophecy; religion; soul; Strauss, Leo**

Further reading: Black 1990; Fakhry 1983; Green 1993; Hughes 2004a; Kreisel 1999 and 2001; Leaman and Nasr 1996; Melamed 2003

Alghazali (1058–1111) was a Muslim theologian, mystic and informed critic of Aristotelian philosophy, especially as propounded by **Alfarabi** and **Avicenna**. Alghazali's *Intentions of the Philosophers* (*Maqāsid al-falāsifa*) offers a summary, but not a refutation, of the main Islamic philosophers, and served as an important introductory text for the basic philosophical curriculum of students. It was translated into Hebrew and was commented on by numerous Jewish philosophers (e.g. **Isaac Albalag, Isaac Polleqar, Moses Narboni,** Isaac ben Shem Tov ibn Shem Tov).

His *Incoherence of the Philosophers* (*Tahāfut al-falāsifa*) is not a simple pietistic attack on philosophy, but provides a reasoned account of what philosophy could and could not do. Although he claims that philosophy had much to offer the various logical and mathematical sciences, Alghazali is critical of philosophers who claim the same certainty in the metaphysical sciences. He accuses philosophers such as Alfarabi and Avicenna of unbelief in three areas: their denial of **creation** *ex nihilo*, their denial of bodily resurrection and their denial that God could not know particulars. Jewish critics of Aristotelianism, most notably **Judah Halevi,** seem to have known well the

Incoherence of the Philosophers and to have used it judiciously in mounting their own critiques.

See **Abravanel, Isaac**; **afterlife**; **Alfarabi**; **Aristotelianism**; **Asharites**; **Avicenna**; **Averroes**; **creation**; **Crescas, Hasdai**; **God, nature of**; **Halevi, Judah**; **Narboni, Moses**; **omnipotence**; **omniscience**; **religious experience**; **religious language**; **theodicy**

Further reading: Fakhry 1983; Leaman and Nasr 1996

allegoresis: Also known as interpretive **allegory**, allegoresis is the interpretation of already existing texts according to extrinsic philosophical or other criteria. In Jewish philosophy, allegoresis is usually reserved for the Bible (and, to a lesser extent, rabbinic texts) in order to find hidden meanings within it that correspond to broader philosophical claims. It was especially popular in biblical commentaries written by philosophers (e.g. those by **Philo, Abraham ibn Ezra, Gersonides**). Philo's claim that Abraham represents a mystical form of philosophy, Hagar general philosophical studies and Ishmael sophistry is a classic form of allegoresis. A further example is Maimonides' interpretation of the story of Adam as really being about the fall of humanity from a state of perfect intellection to one of **imagination** and desire. A more modern example would be **Hermann Cohen**'s reading of the Noahide covenant in the light of **Kant**'s conception of duty. The danger of allegoresis, according to its critics, is that it favours interpretations that are often far removed from both the literal meaning of the text in question and its traditional understanding. Critics fear that allegoresis leads to a decreased commitment to the law.

See **allegory**; **angels**; **apologetics**; **Avicenna**; **Cohen, Hermann**; **gentiles**; **Gersonides**; **halakhah**; **hermeneutics**; **Ibn Ezra, Abraham**; **Ibn Gabirol, Shlomo**; **Ibn Tibbons**; **Jewish people**; **Maimonidean controversies**; **Maimonides,**

Moses; Moses; Philo of Alexandria; religion; religious
language; Sinai; Torah
Further reading: Brague 2003; Eisen 1995; Winston
1985; E.R. Wolfson 1994; H.A. Wolfson 1975

allegory: A literary genre, employed by both philosophers and
non-philosophers, to communicate information in a literary or esoteric manner. Famous examples include Plato's
allegory of the cave, **Abraham ibn Ezra**'s *Living, Son of
Awake* (*Hay ben Meqitz*) and **Maimonides**' allegory of the
palace (*Guide* 3: 51). There is a debate in the secondary
literature as to whether philosophical allegories reveal esoteric information to those who have the capacity to understand, or simply communicate philosophical matters
in a pleasing literary form so that non-philosophers can
understand.
See **aesthetics; allegoresis; Avicenna; Ibn Ezra,
Abraham; Ibn Tufayl; Ikhwan al-Safa; imagination;
kabbalah; metaphor; Neoplatonism; parables; religious
language; Strauss, Leo**
Further reading: Hughes 2004a; Tanenbaum 2002

angels: The majority of medieval Jewish philosophers argued
that God orders and sustains the universe through 'angels', whom they identified with the separate intellects of
Aristotelian **metaphysics**. When the Bible speaks of angels
as playing a role in prophecy, for example, philosophers
such as **Ibn Daud** and **Maimonides** take the term 'angels'
to mean the **Active Intellect**. Other thinkers, most notably
Judah Halevi, disagree with this, and argue that such an
interpretation not only conflicted with the biblical narrative but also makes God's creativity too mechanical or
automatic. Halevi, thus, prefers to regard the angels more
traditionally, as servants of God's **divine will**.
See **Abravanel, Isaac; Active Intellect; allegoresis; Aristotelianism; astronomy; Averroes; cosmology; divine**

attributes; divine will; emanation; God, nature of; Halevi, Judah; intellect; Maimonides, Moses; metaphysics; Neoplatonism; prophecy; religious language

Further reading: Eisen 1995; Frank and Leaman 1997; Kreisel 2001

anti-Semitism: Defined as hatred or hostility directed towards the Jews, anti-Semitism is a modern term, based on racial theory, which replaces the more traditional concept of anti-Judaism. Anti-Semitism, buttressed by the philosophical ideas of **Idealism,** played a large role in regressive laws towards the Jews in Europe, including the prevention of Jewish thinkers and intellectuals from teaching at many European universities. Both **Hegel** and **Kant,** two of the most important and influential figures in modern philosophy, argued that Judaism was an irrational religion and different from Christianity, which they perceived to be the rational religion par excellence (at least in its Protestant form). Once many of these laws had been repelled the spectre of anti-Semitism nevertheless remained, culminating in the **Shoah.** Some philosophers (e.g. **Spinoza**) blame hatred against the Jews as the main cause of Jewish separateness, preventing Jews from forming a national entity. Variations on this position would eventually lead to calls for a separate Jewish homeland. Despite the many forms that anti-Judaism and anti-Semitism have taken over the centuries, all have perhaps paradoxically contributed to Jewish self-understanding.

See **Enlightenment; Geiger, Abraham; Heidegger, Martin; Idealism; Israel, state of; Jewish people; Kant, Immanuel; Mendelssohn, Moses; Rosenzweig, Franz; Shoah, the; Spinoza, Baruch; Wissenschaft des Judentums; Zionism**

Further reading: Frank and Leaman 1997; Katz 1992; Leaman 1997; Mack 2003; Mendes-Flohr and Reinharz 1995; Meyer 1967; Myers 2003

apologetics: Religious apologetics, or the formal defence of
a religion often in response to charges from another
group (either external or internal), usually falls within
the purview of **theology**. Nevertheless, Jewish philosophy represents the synthesis between broader (often
non-Jewish) philosophical ideas and traditional Jewish
sources (namely, the Bible **Talmud**). As such, most Jewish
philosophers work on the assumption that Judaism represents the most perfect religion and that the ideas of
philosophy are expressed most perfectly in it. This was especially in vogue in medieval Christendom, where a number of Jewish thinkers attempted to show the absurdity of
Christian belief in, for example, the Trinity or the figure of
Jesus. It is also evident in **Halevi**'s *Kuzari*, whose subtitle is
'A Defense of the Despised Religion'. Even **Maimonides**'
claim that **Moses** is the most perfect prophet, and by extension the Torah is the most perfect law, is ultimately
based on apologetics. Although not as explicit in modern Jewish philosophy, it is nevertheless possible, on one
level, to read **Hermann Cohen**'s *Religion of Reason out of
the Sources of Judaism* as a Jewish apologetical response
to **Kant**'s claim that Christianity alone was the religion of
reason.

See **Abner of Burgos; Albo, Joseph; chosenness; Cohen,
Hermann; Crescas, Hasdai; Halevi, Judah; Mendelssohn,
Moses; Moses; religion; Torah**

Aristobolus (fl. c. 170s BCE) is considered to be the first
Jewish philosopher whose name we actually know. Other
than his name, however, we know very little about him
except that he worked for the pro-Jewish Ptolemy IV
Philometer (180–145 BCE). Between 176 and 170 BCE
Aristobolus wrote *An Explanation of the Mosaic Scripture*, providing answers to Ptolemy VI Philometer's questions about Judaism. It survives only through fragments

and references to it in the writings of later Church fathers, such as Clement and Eusebius. This work, thus, represents the first recorded attempt of a Jew to make sense of his tradition in light of Greek philosophy. Aristobolus argues that Judaism is superior to other philosophical schools and that Plato and the other Greek philosophers copied from Moses, a claim that would be repeated frequently in the medieval and Renaissance periods.

See **apologetics; Philo of Alexandria; Platonism**
Further reading: Frank and Leaman 1997

Aristotelianism: The rise of Arabic and Jewish Aristotelianism (also known as Peripateticism) is associated with the translation of Greek scientific and philosophical texts into Arabic in tenth-century **Baghdad**. Not all of Aristotle's texts were translated (e.g. his *Politics* was supplanted by Plato's discussion in the *Republic*) and those that were were often read together with various commentaries produced in the late antique period. Many of these commentaries, however, were filtered through various Platonic or Neoplatonic interpretations. An example is the emanative system including the central role of the **Active Intellect** that would form the centrepiece of medieval cosmological speculations. A further example is the **Theology of Aristotle**, which, although it circulated in the name of Aristotle was actually a summary of the Enneads of **Plotinus**.

Both of these examples, among others, succeeded in domesticating pagan or polytheistic Greek thought into a more monotheistic framework (e.g. the One = God). Many of the famous Islamic philosophers (e.g. **Alfarabi, Averroes, Avicenna**) wrote commentaries on works of Aristotle, especially the *Organon* (the various logical texts, which included the *Rhetoric* and the *Poetics*).

Central themes of Aristotelianism that would play an important role in Jewish philosophy include: **ethics**; the four causes (material, formal, efficient and final); **logic;** and the various natural sciences. Since Aristotelianism tended to operate with a different set of assumptions about the world, the individual and the nature of human happiness, it often conflicted with the traditional claims of Judaism. Moreover, since Aristotelianism was the dominant strand in the thought of most medieval Jewish philosophers, those critical of philosophy mounted attacks against it (e.g. **Halevi, Crescas, Isaac Abravanel**). As a scientific world-view, Aristotelianism was gradually replaced in the sixteenth and seventeenth centuries.

See **Abravanel, Isaac; Active Intellect; Alexander of Aphrodisias; Alfarabi; Alghazali; astronomy; Averroes; Avicenna; Baghdad; celestial spheres; creation; Crescas, Hasdai; emanation; epistemology; eternity; form; Gersonides; God, arguments for the existence of; God, knowledge of; Halevi, Judah; happiness; Ibn Daud, Abraham; Ibn Tibbons; intellect; logic; Maimonidean controversies; Maimonides, Moses; metaphysics; miracles; Neoplatonism; physics; Platonism; Plotinus; political philosophy; Scholasticism; Themistius; Theology of Aristotle**

Further reading: Black 1990; Eisen 1995; Fakhry 1983; Frank and Leaman 1997 and 2003; Guttmann 1964; Harvey 1998; Kraemer 1991; Kreisel 1999; Reines 1970; Rudavsky 2000; Silver 1965; Tirosh-Samuelson 2003; H.A. Wolfson 1957

Asharites: An important theological school in medieval Islam. Their eponymous founder, al-Ashari (d. 935), was critical of the rationalising tendencies of the **Mutazilites.** Yet rather than repudiate their form of systematic theology entirely (as others, most notably Ibn Hanbal, had done), the Asharites argued that the essential attributes of God (e.g. knowledge, power, life) subsist eternally in God's essence, but are not, as the Mutazilites maintained, identical with this essence. For the Asharites, the mode of predicating attributes of God cannot be known. For example, when the Koran says 'God's hand', hand cannot be a metaphor for God's providence, but that God literally has a 'hand', only in a manner that the human mind cannot fathom.

The Asharites also criticised the Mutazilite concept of individuals as free agents, and instead argued that God's power was absolute and his decrees irreversible. This led subsequent Asharites to develop an elaborate atomic theory, in which everything in this world is made up of atoms and accidents that are continuously maintained or destroyed by God. Asharism would eventually become the orthodox theological school in Islam.

There is little evidence that there were Jewish Asharites, yet the various debates between the Asharites and the Mutazilites played a large role in the emergence of Jewish philosophy as can be witnessed in the theological-philosophical thought of **Saadia Gaon**.

See **atomism; determinism; divine attributes; free will; God, knowledge of; God, nature of; kalam; Mutazilites; omnipotence; omniscience; providence; religion**

Further reading: Fakhry 1983; Leaman and Nasr 1996; Pines 1997

astrology: A rabbinic tradition states that 'Israel has no astrological sign', meaning that Jews should not believe in astrology for themselves, but not necessarily for other nations. Many Jewish philosophers tend to agree, faulting astrology for putting too strong an emphasis on **determinism**. Two of the most severe critics of astrology were **Maimonides** and **Isaac Polleqar**, both of whom try to undermine the scientific foundations of astrology.

Those philosophers who do emphasise astrology, for example, **Abraham bar Hiyya** and **Abraham ibn Ezra,** tend to be influenced by **Neoplatonism** (as opposed to **Aristotelianism**) especially the notion that this world is made in the image of the celestial world and that, as a result, the latter influences the former. Ibn Ezra in particular argues that Jews and the land of Israel are under the influence of Saturn, and he interprets key biblical events in light of this (e.g. the golden calf as an attempt to harness divine influence; the scapegoat on Yom Kippur as an attempt to appease the anger of Mars). The fourteenth century witnessed a renaissance in astrology undoubtedly brought about by the great number of supercommentaries written on Ibn Ezra, in addition to the growing influence of **kabbalah**.

See **Abner of Burgos; astronomy; bar Hiyya, Abraham; determinism; emanation; free will; Ibn Ezra, Abraham; kabbalah; Neoplatonism; Polleqar, Isaac**

Further reading: Brague 2003; Frank and Leaman 1997; Goodman 1992; Sirat 1985

astronomy: A belief about God is never an independent belief, for God stands in some form of relationship to the world as its creator. What we believe about God then cannot be independent from what we believe about the universe. Within this context, astronomy is the study of the movement of the celestial bodies and the laws that govern such movements. According to Aristotelian astronomy, our world is at the centre of the universe, with all the planets moving around it in solid spheres. The universe is generated and ordered by means of the separate intellects that emanate from the First Cause. **Maimonides** argues that certain knowledge of the celestial world was impossible for humans. Yet **Gersonides**, probably the most important astronomer in medieval Jewish philosophy, claims that he had arrived at such knowledge. For him, such knowledge confirms the **creation** of the universe out of pre-existent matter. He bases this, in general, on three types of arguments: (1) teleological facts about the universe; (2) contingent facts about the universe; and (3) the absurdity of the concept of eternity.

In the contemporary period, the Aristotelian position can no longer be taken seriously by anyone who accepts the validity of science as a way of knowing reality. In other words, modern astronomy limits its methodology to a discussion of efficient causes and maintains that events in natural history are not goal oriented. For this reason, modern Jewish philosophers (e.g. Norbert Samuelson) struggle to make sense of traditional doctrines in the light of contemporary sciences that deal with the origin of the universe (e.g. astrophysics).

See **angels; Aristotelianism; astrology; bar Hiyya, Abraham; cosmology; creation; emanation; eternity; Genesis; Gersonides; intellect; metaphysics; nature; pantheism; reason; transcendence**

Further reading: Eisen 1995; Frank and Leaman 1997 and 2003; Harvey 1998; Nasr 1993; Rudavsky 2000

atomism: Developed in the fifth century BCE by Leucippus and Democritus, atomism is a cosmological and physical theory that argues that atoms are the ultimate constituents of physical bodies, and that all physical properties could be understood as the result of various collisions and regroupings of such atoms. Atomism proved particularly popular among the **kalam** schools of Muslim theology, especially the **Asharites** and the **Mutazilites**. Both of these schools believed that all bodies were composed of atoms in which accidents reside. This theory was usually coupled with a rejection of natural causality and the affirmation of **occasionalism,** or the continuous creation of the universe. The Mutazilites, however, argued that God was only the Cause of bodies, but that the actual accidents inhering in them were the products of these bodies either naturally (e.g. fire as the cause of smoke) or voluntarily (e.g. knowledge, willing).

Between the tenth and eleventh centuries, atomism seems to have been the dominant scientific paradigm for explaining the physical universe. It was, however, gradually replaced by **Aristotelianism**. Atomism, minus the occassionalism, seems to have been popular among **Karaite** thinkers. More recently, Newtonian physics is predicated on the premise that the universe is regarded as constituted of particles responsible for the formation of complex and compound entities. Modern theories that deal, in one way or another, with increasingly complex theories of atoms include theoretical chemistry and quantum mechanics.

See **Aristotelianism; Asharites; cosmology; creation; God, nature of; kalam; Karaites; matter; nature; occassionalism; Mutazilites; Saadia Gaon**

Further reading: Fakhry 1983; Frank and Leaman 1997 and 2003; Leaman and Nasr 1996; Pines 1997

autonomy: According to **Kant,** human reason is an autonomous source for principles of conduct; namely, morality must be based on reason and not subservience to divine fiat in the form of external revelation. Every person thus has the ability to know what morality requires and must act on this knowledge. Kant is particularly critical of Judaism, which he regards as the stereotype of a legislated, heteronomous religion, as opposed to one based on reason (e.g. Protestant Christianity). This concept of autonomy poses difficulties for traditional Judaism, which locates **knowledge of God** in external **revelation**.

One of the first Jewish philosophers to interpret Judaism through the prism of autonomy is **Moses Mendelssohn**. For him, human reason is autonomous when it comes to eternal truths (e.g. existence, unity and eternality of God) but that the revealed laws and practices of Judaism are necessary and rational even if we are not entirely sure how. This creates as many questions as it solves. Is belief in the **Torah** simply taken on faith (which would imply a heteronomous position)? Why would God single out the Jews not to eat shellfish, but allow other people to eat it?

Hermann Cohen, on the contrary, argues that the goal of religion, whether natural or revealed, is to get us to choose morality for its own sake. Revelation, for him, is not a supernatural event, but is tantamount to the creation of reason in humanity: Jews must sanctify themselves in order to establish a relationship with God and not blindly follow an arbitrary set of **commandments.**

Subsequent Jewish philosophers, influenced more by **Existentialism** than **Idealism,** tend to focus on autonomy and **ethics** not so much as ideas but as encounters. **Buber,** for example, claims that the nature of the **covenant** demands that humans should not slavishly follow the commandments, but engage in a dialectical relationship with each other and with God. Human autonomy is a central component of the religious life only now it is not based on objectively valid moral principles but on the uniqueness of individual encounters.

See **anti-Semitism; Buber, Martin; Cohen, Hermann; commandments; covenant; Existentialism; God, knowledge of; God, nature of; halakhah; Idealism; Kant, Immanuel; Levinas, Emmanuel; Mendelssohn, Moses; Post-Modernism; revelation; Torah**

Further reading: Gordon 2003; Harris 1991; Samuelson 1989; Seeskin 2001; Tirosh-Samuelson 2003

Averroes (1126–98), royal physician and chief judge, was arguably the most important of all the Islamic philosophers. He wrote the most extensive commentaries to all of Aristotle's works with the exception of the *Politics*, although he did write a paraphrase of Plato's *Republic* that survives in a Hebrew translation. Most of Averroes' commentaries were also subsequently translated into Hebrew, and many Jewish philosophers (e.g. **Gersonides, Moses Narboni**) wrote supercommentaries to these works. He also wrote an important justification for engaging in philosophical speculation, *The Decisive Treatise* (*Fasl al-maqāl*), which argues on theological grounds that the Koran demands reflection on the natural and supernatural worlds. This is Averroes' response to the perennial clash between **reason** and **religion** in the Middle Ages.

Averroes is also critical of **Alghazali**'s attack against **Aristotelianism**. Indeed Averroes wrote a treatise, *The Incoherence of the Incoherence* (*Tahāfut al-tahāfut*), to counter Alghazali's own *Incoherence of the Philosophers*. Whereas Alghazali claimed that the world is created out of nothing, Averroes argues that the concept of an eternal will that brings the world into being in time is a contradiction presupposing an infinite amount of time in which God would have done nothing. Therefore, God cannot create the world in time unless he himself is in time, a proposition that Alghazali and the **Asharites** denied. Averroes instead opts for the eternal production of the universe, in which God brings form and matter together in a continuous way. This latter position would exert tremendous influence on the so-called 'Jewish-Averroists', such as **Isaac Albalag** and **Moses Narboni**.

See **Abner of Burgos; Albalag, Isaac; Alghazali; Aristotelianism; Asharites; Avicenna; eternity; Gersonides; Ibn Bajja; Ibn Tibbons; Ibn Tufayl; logic; metaphysics; Narboni, Moses; Polleqar, Isaac; religion; Scholasticism**

Further reading: Fakhry 1983; Leaman and Nasr 1996

Avicenna (980–1037), one of the most important of the Islamic philosophers, was the author of numerous philosophical, scientific, medical and quasi-mystical treatises. The most important of these many diverse writings is *The Healing (al-Shifā')*, a fifteen-volume compendium, much of which is written as a **commentary** to Aristotle, covering the whole range of philosophical sciences known in his day. Unlike his contemporary **Alfarabi**, Avicenna is not particularly interested in either **ethics** or **politics**. Instead, he devotes most of his interest to **metaphysics** and **logic**. Avicenna argues that 'Being' is the first concept acquired by the mind. Here, Avicenna uses his 'flying man' argument. Let us imagine a grown man, created suddenly, with eyes covered, suspended in space, and whose limbs do not touch one other. Such a man, according to Avicenna, would know that he exists. Knowledge of being is therefore immediate and no other notion is prior to it.

Avicenna's metaphysics is also predicated on two important distinctions: that between **essence and existence,** and that between necessary and contingent existence. Essence is the definition of a thing (e.g. man as a rational bipedal animal); existence, in contrast, is superadded to essence. In like manner, something is said to be necessary if its non-existence would imply an absurdity, while something is said to be contingent if no such absurdity would follow. (The first Jewish philosopher to employ this distinction seems to be **Abraham ibn Ezra.**) Necessary existence is further subdivided into that which is necessary through itself and that which is necessary through another. That which is necessary through another requires a cause for its existence, while that which is necessary through itself does not. Because that which is necessary in itself does not require another for its existence, its existence is part of its very essence.

This distinction leads Avicenna to develop his proof for God's existence: all contingent beings require, for their existence, a being necessary through itself. This proof would be used subsequently by **Maimonides** and Aquinas. Some of Avicenna's work, especially that written near the end of his life, is more interested in mystical or intuitive ways of grasping the truth.

See **Active Intellect; Alfarabi; Aristotelianism; Averroes; essence and existence; eternity; God, arguments for the existence of; God, nature of; Halevi, Judah; Ibn Ezra, Abraham; Ibn Tufayl; logic; Maimonides, Moses; metaphysics; mysticism; Neoplatonism; rational mysticism; Scholasticism**

Further reading: Fakhry 1983; Hughes 2004a; Leaman and Nasr 1996

B

Baeck, Leo (1873–1956) was a Reform rabbi and theologian, a survivor of the **Shoah,** and the leading liberal thinker of his time. For Baeck, the evil of the Shoah was the direct result of freedom of choice, in which people chose not to do what was ethical. He agrees with **Moses Mendelssohn** that Judaism is not a religion of **dogma,** but one of divine legislation (e.g. **commandments**). Following **Hermann Cohen,** Baeck locates the essence of Judaism in ethical **monotheism,** while downplaying the ritual acts of the tradition. In his later writings, however, he adds to this the element of mystery that is inherent in Judaism. This mystery, which functions as an awareness of the holy, is expressed through the commandments. It is in the tension between history and the holy, Baeck contends, that every Jew ultimately finds him- or herself.

See **Cohen, Hermann; commandments; dogma; evil, problem of; God, nature of; Mendelssohn, Moses; monotheism; Shoah, the**

Baghdad was in the ninth century the centre of translation activity in the Islamic Empire. In 830 the caliph al-Mamun founded the famous 'House of Wisdom' to serve as both a library and an institute of translation. There, many Greek philosophical and scientific texts were translated from Greek and Syriac into Arabic. Hunayn ibn Ishaq (d. 873), called by many the greatest figure in the history of translation, and his disciples translated texts such as Aristotle's *Physics, Metaphysics, Posterior Analytics* and *Nicomachean Ethics* (including various late antique commentaries on such texts), in addition to synopses of Plato's *Sophist, Parmenides, Laws* and *Republic*. An excellent contemporaneous catalogue of the philosophical books that the Islamic and Jewish philosophers would have had access to is found in the *Fihrist* of al-Nadim (d. c. 1047).

See **Alexander of Aphrodisias; Aristotelianism; commentary; Neoplatonism; Plotinus; Theology of Aristotle; Themistius**
Further reading: Gutas 1998

bar Hiyya, Abraham (1065–after 1136) lived in Barcelona, where he worked in the court of Alfonso I. He was also the first philosopher to compose a philosophical treatise in **Hebrew**. He wrote works on **mathematics** and **astronomy**; however, his two most important works are the *Scroll of the Revealer* (*Megillat ha-Megalleh*) and the *Meditation of the Sad Soul* (*Hegyon ha-Nefesh ha-Azuvah*). The latter work argues that the **Torah** teaches science and, perhaps because of this, he tries to mesh the Neoplatonic and biblical accounts of **creation**.

According to bar Hiyya, God first created things to exist potentially; creation, then, is the actualisation of this potentiality, with time coming into existence with the motion caused by the **celestial spheres**. Bar Hiyya puts the nation of Israel, and not humans in general, at the pinnacle of creation, a theme that **Judah Halevi** would subsequently pick up on and develop. According to his psychology, the human soul is comprised of three faculties: vegetative, animal and rational. Only the third of these souls is eternal, and it is engaged in a constant battle with the lower two souls that seek to mire it in their desires and passions. The *Scroll of the Revealer* is essentially a messianic treatise, in which bar Hiyya attempts to calculate the date of the Messiah's coming based on biblical verses and the inner working of history.

See **celestial spheres; cosmology; creation; Genesis; Halevi, Judah; Hebrew; matter; Messianic Era; Neoplatonism; religious language; soul**

Further reading: Frank and Leaman 1997; Guttmann 1964; Sirat 1985

belief: Judaism is in theory an orthoprax as opposed to an orthodox religion, stressing correct intention and action over correct belief. The question of what must Jews believe, related to the question of **dogma**, became important only in the medieval period owing to (1) the contact with Islam and (2) **Karaite** sectarianism. The earliest philosopher to develop foundational beliefs that all Jews must accept is **Maimonides** and his thirteen principles of faith (e.g. **God** is one; God is eternal; **prophecy; Torah** from heaven; **Messianic Era,** resurrection of the dead). Yet, in *Guide* 3: 28, Maimonides argues that beliefs are only politically necessary, but need not be philosophically true. An important question arises: does Maimonides regard beliefs in a way that resembles Plato's concept of 'noble lies'?

Increasingly in the fourteenth and fifteenth centuries, undoubtedly brought about by the increased polemics between Jews and Christians, the question of belief became important. Many of the most important thinkers develop their own principles of beliefs to counter the thirteen principles of Maimonides (e.g. **Hasdai Crescas, Joseph Albo** and **Isaac Abravanel**). Although many of these thinkers disagree on what the core beliefs of Judaism should be, the tendency is to regard beliefs not simply as minimum requirements, but as foundational principles from which all other secondary principles can be derived.

In the sixteenth century, the formulation of principles of faith fell out of favour, but returns in the late eighteenth and early nineteenth century as Jewish intellectuals and reformers try to define Judaism in various ways based on **Enlightenment** principles and, in so doing, attempt to differentiate these new forms of Judaism from what is perceived to be too traditional or pre-modern.

See **Abner of Burgos; Abravanel, Isaac; Albo, Joseph; apologetics; commandments; covenant; Crescas, Hasdai; dogma; Enlightenment; Jewish people; Maimonides, Moses; Messianic Era; Moses; prophecy; Sinai; Torah**
Further reading: Kellner 1986

Buber, Martin (1878–1965) was born in Vienna to a religiously observant family, was part of the intellectual and spiritual leadership of German Jewry prior to the **Shoah,** and subsequent Professor of Social Philosophy at the Hebrew University in Jerusalem. Buber is best known for his *I and Thou* (*Ich und Du*), a landmark work that emphasises the importance of dialogue between individuals as leading to authenticity.

Buber differentiates between two types of relationships, the I–Thou and the I–It. The first relationship is direct and takes place with another, leading to the formation of self ('I'); the second, by contrast, is not reciprocal, but impersonal, in which the other is regarded as an object. The I–Thou relationship is not an objective ethical code, but a way of responding to another based on their status as a genuine person. This involves the full acceptance of the other as he or she is without attempting to change him or her for our own selfish reasons. The I–Thou relationship is so difficult to establish, however, because it often becomes, consciously or otherwise, an I–It relationship, in which we try to manipulate the other. Moreover, Buber does not expect us to have an I–Thou relationship with everyone we encounter. Certainly I cannot have, for example, an I–Thou relationship with the person from whom I buy a car, but I must still treat that person with respect.

The I–Thou relationship also plays an important role in the religious life, the goal of which is to enter into a dialogue with God. Only this dialogue with God is not direct, but occurs as we enter into appropriate relationships with others and the world of nature. In his later thought, much of it written after the Shoah, Buber begins to speak of the eclipse of God, something that would have major repercussions on the I–Thou relationship. Buber is critical of orthodox Judaism's propensity to regard the **halakhah** as legislation as opposed to dialogue. He nevertheless finds as a shining example of the ideal type of relationship that an individual should have with God in his highly romanticised reading of Hasidic, or 'Ultra-orthodox', Judaism of Eastern Europe. For him, this form of Judaism represents the true creativity and authenticity that was to be found in religion.

See **Cohen, Hermann; ethics; Existentialism; God, knowledge of; halakhah; Hegel, Georg Wilhelm Friedrich; Heidegger, Martin; Israel, state of; Jewish**

People; Levinas, Emmanuel; nature; pantheism; Rosenzweig, Franz; Shoah, the; Soloveitchik, Joseph; Zionism

Further reading: Frank and Leaman 1997; Friedman 2002; Myers 2003; Samuelson 1989; Seeskin 2001

celestial spheres: Medieval astronomy was predicated on the notion of **emanation**, in which God's self-intellection leads to the subsequent production of a number of separate intellects (usually regarded as ten in number). From each one of the celestial intellects emanates a celestial sphere, beginning with the diurnal sphere of the first intellect and finishing with the sphere of the moon that is associated with the tenth intellect, better known as the **Active Intellect**. The celestial spheres thus function as the orbits in which exist the separate intellects. According to Aristotelian science, especially as elaborated upon by **Alexander of Aphrodisias**, it is the perpetual movement of the spheres that is responsible for the various natural forces in the sublunar world, thereby ensuring the preservation of the terrestrial species. The motion of the celestial spheres then is associated with the concept of divine **providence** (this was, e.g., the opinion of Maimonides).

See **Active Intellect; Alexander of Aphrodisias; angels; Aristotelianism; astronomy; corporeality; cosmology; creation; emanation; eternity; God, nature of; intellect; Maimonides, Moses; matter; metaphysics; Neoplatonism**

chosenness: The concept of chosenness looms large in Jewish theology: God picked the Jewish people from among all of the nations on earth to be his chosen people, receive his **Torah**, etc. Philosophically this creates a problem: how can such a particularistic argument be supported by the universal claims of philosophy? If human perfection is based on intellectual ability, how can a Jew unskilled in philosophy be 'chosen' over a pagan like Plato or a Muslim like **Alfarabi**? For informed critics of philosophy, such as **Halevi** or **Isaac Abravanel**, this does not pose a problem as such, because the giving of the Torah on **Sinai** is regarded as sufficient proof that the Jewish people possess an inherited essence that makes them qualitatively different from (i.e. superior to) other groups.

For philosophers, however, the problem cannot be solved so easily. **Maimonides** as an Aristotelian, tellingly and not surprisingly, makes no mention of the chosenness of the Jewish people in his thirteen principles, nor does he spend any time in the *Guide* on this topic. He does mention it, however, in his *Epistle to Yemen* (*Iggeret Teman*), where he links chosenness to God's promise to Abraham in Genesis 17: 1–8. Although Maimonides here seems to be less interested in philosophical claims than in countering Muslim claims that Ishmael, as opposed to Isaac, is the true inheritor of the **covenant** that God established with Abraham.

A more substantial discussion can be found in the work of **Gersonides**, who contends that owing to the righteousness and intellectual perfection of Abraham, the generation at Sinai inherited his **providence**. This providence is subsequently inherited by the generations after Sinai, thereby establishing an intimate covenantal relationship between God and the Jewish people.

In the modern period, **Franz Rosenzweig** resignifies chosenness as Judaism's sublimity of isolation and its freedom from the false attachments of land, state and history. Such features, according to him, have enabled the Jews, unlike other peoples, to be less concerned with mundane affairs than with religious authenticity.

See **Abravanel, Isaac; Alfarabi; covenant; ethics; Gersonides; halakhah; Halevi, Judah; happiness; Jewish people; Maimonides, Moses; prophecy; Rosenzweig, Franz; Sinai; Torah; Zionism**

Further reading: Eisen 1995; Gordon 2003; Harris 1991; Lawee 2001; Lobel 2000; Myers 2003; Tirosh-Samuelson 2003; E.R. Wolfson 1994

Cohen, Hermann (1842–1918) was a mathematician and a prominent follower of the thought of **Immanuel Kant**. He founded the Marburg school of thought that was responsible for reviving Kant's ethical principles. Two of Cohen's most famous students were **Martin Buber** and **Franz Rosenzweig**. Although Cohen was able to become a professor at a German university, he frequently had to counter the charges of **anti-Semitism**. His *A Public Declaration concerning the Jewish Question* (*Ein Bekenntis zur Judenfrage*) argues for the total integration of German Jews into German society, but in such a manner that they take their Judaism seriously. He also responds to the charge of Jewish particularism by claiming that Judaism's **chosenness** has universal scope. Even though he is not particularly interested in Judaism in his early writings, Cohen becomes increasingly preoccupied with Judaism and attempts to use Kantian principles to explore some of the central features of its teachings.

Cohen's most famous work, the rather enigmatic *Religion of Reason out of the Sources of Judaism* (*Religion der Vernunft aus den Quellen des Judentums*, published posthumously in 1919), is an attempt to rehabilitate Judaism in light of Kant's critique of Judaism as being a partial or heteronomous religion because it was composed of nothing more than statutory laws. In formulating his response, Cohen emphasises the concept of duty, a concept that Kant had argued as foundational to religion. The laws of ancient Israel are not specific to only one people, the Jews, but are applicable to all of humanity. Unlike medieval thinkers, Cohen equates the knowledge of God not with science or **metaphysics** but with the duty of fulfilling the moral laws.

Influenced by German **Idealism**, Cohen regards Judaism not as a historical religion but as the ongoing awareness of moral reason. God is the author of this moral reason not in the sense that Shakespeare is the author of *Hamlet*, but in the sense that a cause is the author of consequences that follow from it. Yet, much like **Maimonides**, Cohen claims that a religion must be more than just abstract principles; it also needs rituals, symbols and myths to help practitioners understand, conceptualise and follow this moral law. These rituals, symbols and myths though are not irrational impositions of an arbitrary will, but necessary prerequisites for obeying a rational will. For Cohen, discovering the demands of moral reason is tantamount to knowledge of God's will.

See **autonomy; Buber, Martin; commandments; covenant; divine will; ethics; God, knowledge of; God, nature of; halakhah; Idealism; Jewish people; Kant, Immanuel; Maimonides, Moses; monotheism; Noahide laws; Rosenzweig, Franz**

Further reading: Batnitzky 2000; Frank and Leaman 1997; Gordon 2003; Mack 2003; Myers 2003; Samuelson 1989; Seeskin 2001

commandments: The divine commandments (in Hebrew they are known as *mitzvot*) are, according to Jewish theology, the *sine qua non* of Jewish life. Following the commandments leads to the perfection of the Jewish people, whereas failure to perform the commandments leads to collective punishment. Commandments run the gamut from prohibition against murder to prohibitions against eating milk with meat. Philosophically, the former is easy to justify, whereas the latter is not. If human **happiness** is all about intellectual perfection, then how does my having a cheeseburger contribute to such happiness? Philosophers, perhaps unfairly, are often criticised for creating a system that either downplays the commandments or leads people to ignore them.

Saadia Gaon was one of the earliest thinkers to analyse the commandments from a rationalist point of view. For him, commandments are divided into two categories: those of reason and those of revelation. The former constitute prohibitions against murder, adultery, theft, etc., whereas the latter include laws governing, for example, the Sabbath, holidays and dietary laws. Both are equally important and both are necessary for happiness and salvation. Saadia argues, for example, that reason tells us that we need a Sabbath, but not how we should keep it.

Maimonides contends that all of the commandments have rational reasons. These reasons are related to their purpose. Maimonides, thus, understands the commandments teleologically, and it is the goal of every believer to discover the rational purposes behind them. The commandments were given to humanity for their intellectual perfection. (For example, circumcision is meant to dull the sexual appetite.) This creates a problem, though: if it is the goal of every believer to understand the reasons behind the commandments, what happens when one does this? Does one no longer need them? **Gersonides**, following Maimonides, claims that the **Torah** (and, thus, all the commandments) embodies the perfect law, revealing to humanity the path to happiness.

In modern Jewish philosophy, **Rosenzweig** argues that the commandments provide the meaningful structures for Jewish life. Adherence to the commandments is what ultimately leads practitioners to understand what it means to live in eternity (i.e. ahistorically). **Buber,** however, contends that the commandments have the potential to blur the living relationship that the believer must have with God.

See **allegoresis; autonomy; belief; Buber, Martin; conversion; covenant; ethics; Gersonides; God, knowledge of; halakhah; happiness; Jewish people; Levinas, Emmanuel; Maimonidean controversies; Maimonides, Moses; prayer; prophecy; religion; religious experience; Rosenzweig, Franz; Saadia Gaon; sin; Torah**

Further reading: Eisen 1995; Feiner 2002; Kaplan 1996; Kellner 1986; Lobel 2000; Samuelson 2002; Seeskin 2001; Tirosh-Samuelson 2003; Twersky 1980

commentary: The writing of commentary to an authoritative text is a basic activity in the Jewish tradition. For example, **midrash** and the **Talmud** essentially function as commentaries to the Bible, expanding it, drawing out its significances, reading it intertextually, etc. Furthermore, an important activity in philosophy, especially in late antiquity, was the writing of commentaries to the texts of Plato and Aristotle.

There is an unfair assumption that the genre of commentary is inherently conservative, the genre used by lesser-known thinkers to work out philosophical issues that were expounded (perhaps opaquely) by the 'great men'. In fact, the opposite is often the case: the commentary allowed creative individuals to develop often very original philosophical ideas, but in such a way that they did not appear so because they were embedded in the great names of the past. In medieval Islamic philosophy, the majority of the great philosophers (e.g. **Alfarabi, Avicenna, Averroes**) wrote most of their original works in the form of commentary to either the work of Plato or Aristotle (and, to a lesser extent, other thinkers of late antiquity).

Jewish philosophy is essentially the writing of commentary to the **Torah** in order to understand it rationally. This commentary writing can either be explicit (e.g. in the line-by-line commentaries of **Abraham ibn Ezra** or **Gersonides**) or implicit (e.g. in the exposition of certain words or concepts in the writings of **Maimonides** or **Franz Rosenzweig**).

See **Alfarabi**; **allegoresis**; **Averroes**; **Avicenna**; **Genesis**; **hermeneutics**; **Ibn Ezra, Abraham**; **Maimonides, Moses**; **parables**; **reason**; **religion**; **religious language**; **Talmud**; **theology**; **Torah**

Further reading: Eisen 1995 and 2004; Harris 1991; Lawee 2001

compatibilism and **incompatibilism:** Compatibilism is the position that claims that God's knowledge of future contingents is compatible with human freedom to choose. Most Jewish philosophers adopted some form of compatibilism, claiming that God's knowledge of future events in no way impedes human freedom. **Gersonides**, for example, argues that God knows the ordered nature or essence of future contingents – for example, whether I shall go in or stay out tomorrow – but does not know what alternative will become actual. The opposite of compatibilism is incompatibilism, which claims that God's knowledge is not compatible with human freedom, a position that is not particularly popular in Jewish philosophy.

See **Abner of Burgos**; **Asharites**; **autonomy**; **determinism**; **free will**; **Gersonides**; **God, knowledge of**; **God, nature of**; **kalam**; **Mutazilites**; **Narboni, Moses**; **omnipotence**; **omniscience**; **providence**

Further reading: Frank and Leaman 1997 and 2003

conversion: One of the most common charges levelled against Jewish philosophy in both the medieval and modern periods is that the universal claims of reason weaken a Jew's commitment to the particularism embodied in the **halakhah**. Although philosophers would say that intellectual perfection is synonymous with religious perfection, critics respond by claiming that philosophy, in stressing scientific over religious knowledge, marginalises religious **faith** in favour of individual **happiness**. In the aftermath of anti-Jewish riots in the fourteenth century and especially after the expulsion of the Jews from Spain in 1492, for example, critics such as **Hasdai Crescas** argued that Jews influenced by philosophy were more likely to convert to Christianity owing to philosophy's allegorisation of the law. **Franz Rosenzweig** originally felt the need to convert to Christianity but thought that before he did this he should properly understand his own religious tradition. In 1913 he had a form of **religious experience** that transformed him: no longer did he regard Judaism as preparatory to Christianity; instead he devoted the rest of his life to a philosophical elucidation of Judaism.

See **Abner of Burgos; Alfarabi; allegoresis; allegory; anti-Semitism; belief; chosenness; commandments; Crescas, Hasdai; determinism; dogma; Enlightenment; halakhah; happiness; Jewish people; Kant, Immanuel; Maimonidean controversies; Mendelssohn, Moses; Rosenzweig, Franz; Spinoza, Baruch; Strauss, Leo; Wissenschaft des Judentums; Zionism**

corporeality: The quality of being physical or existing in matter. In the sublunar or terrestrial world it is corporeality that is ultimately responsible for the generation and corruption of individuals. In medieval psychology, it is the union of the soul, which is incorporeal, with the body that is the main source of temptation for the individual and, if the individual does not engage in philosophical study, the body will ultimately dominate the soul. The goal of philosophy, therefore, is to disengage from the corporeality of this world in order to (1) return one's soul to its true celestial home (as in **Neoplatonism**) or (2) engage in pure thinking which constitutes the formal end of the human species (as in **Aristotelianism**).

See **Aristotelianism; Asharites; atomism; cosmology; emanation; ethics; evil, problem of; form; happiness; kalam; matter; Mutazilites; nature; Neoplatonism; physics**

cosmology: In effect, any attempt to give a reasoned account of the universe or cosmos. The two most important individuals in the articulation of cosmology in Jewish philosophy were Plato and Aristotle. Plato argued that a demiurge or divine craftsman was responsible for bringing order to the universe. Aristotle who sought to provide a plausible causal explanation of the planetary motions provided the most important theory, indeed one that would last for close to 1800 years. He posited a series of fifty-five rotating spheres that move owing to the rotation of an immanent mover or soul. These motions are eternal and therefore unlike motions that exist on earth. This theory, as interpreted by the likes of **Alexander of Aphrodisias**, would inform the theory of **emanation** that was basic to medieval and early modern science.

In Jewish philosophy, any theory of the universe has to take into account the nature of the relationship between the cosmos and God. For early Jewish rationalists, such as **Saadia Gaon**, the universe is a wilful **creation** of God and, therefore, contingent upon him (which he attempted to prove based on the argument from design). Later Aristotelians, such as **ibn Daud** and **Maimonides**, consider cosmology to be an imprecise science owing to the finitude of the human intellect and its inability to acquire certain knowledge beyond the sphere of the moon.

Gersonides, however, disagrees and claims to know with certainty the origin of the universe. Modern cosmology is based on the 'big bang' theory and the idea of an expanding universe, thereby making it less amenable to a religious understanding owing to its inherent spontaneity and its inability to posit something beyond our finite universe.

See **Active Intellect; angels; Aristotelianism; Asharites; Averroes; creation; divine will; emanation; eternity; Genesis; Gersonides; God, knowledge of; God, nature of; kalam; Krochmal, Nachman; Maimonides, Moses; Mutazilites; Neoplatonism; pantheism; Platonism; Plotinus; Rosenzweig, Franz; Saadia Gaon; soul**

Further reading: Brague 2003; Feldman 2003; Goodman 1992; Gordon 2003; Harvey 1998; Hughes 2004a; Nasr 1993; Rudavsky 2000; E.R. Wolfson 1994

covenant: The personal God of rabbinic Judaism has a special relationship with one group of people, Israel. This relationship is understood in terms of an eternal covenant, a perpetual interaction that cannot be broken. The covenantal relationship is spelled out in the **Torah**, and reward and punishment is understood in terms of the ability or inability of Israel to fulfill its terms of the covenantal relationship. The concept of covenant, even if redefined, plays a large role in Jewish philosophy and it succeeds in separating it markedly from Greek philosophy. Whereas the latter is based on human effort through, for example, the acquisition of virtues, the former is ultimately grounded in the relationship that one has to God and, through him, to others.

Although medieval and modern philosophers tend to redefine the personal God of rabbinic Judaism, they nevertheless take the nature of the relationship between God and Israel seriously. Some modern Jewish thinkers,

JEWISH PHILOSOPHY A–Z   45

living in the aftermath of the **Shoah,** have, however, begun to rethink this term.

See **belief; commandments; dogma; God, nature of; halakhah; happiness; Jewish people; Moses; prophecy; religion; religious language; revelation; Sinai; Torah**

Further reading: Eisen 1995; Kaplan 1996; Kellner 1986; Leaman 1997; Samuelson 1989 and 2002; Seeskin 1990 and 2001

creation: Creation, which establishes God's relationship to the world, is central to the biblical world-view. Belief in the **halakhah** ultimately depends upon God's ability to act supernaturally and directly in **history.** Creation thus makes an entire gamut of other traditional beliefs possible (e.g. resurrection of the dead, **prophecy, Messianic Era**). Creation was often contrasted with the thesis of the **eternity** of the world, upon which much of Aristotelian science was based. Since the majority of medieval philosophers were indebted to **Aristotelianism,** they were often accused of believing in the world's eternality (even if they explicitly argued for creation) and thus denying traditional beliefs. There were essentially two ways to understand the 'traditional' account of creation (for a non-traditional account, see **creation, eternal** below):

1. Creation *ex nihilo* (from nothing). This is the opinion of individuals as diverse as **Saadia Gaon, Joseph Albo, Hasdai Crescas** and **Isaac Abravanel,** all of whom claim that creation *ex nihilo* can be proven from observing the mundane world. For all of these individuals, the world's existence is derivative and cannot exist without God wilfully bringing it into existence. Time, as an accident of motion, is also regarded as created. Proponents of this position contend that

this theory fits most closely with the first chapter of **Genesis**.

2. Creation from pre-existent matter. This position contends that God actively created the world by bringing form and order to eternal matter. This is most often associated with the thought of Plato. A variation on this theme is provided by **Gersonides**, who holds that the world is created from a preexistent and formless body upon which God imprinted a lower form (which receives the four elemental forms) and a higher form (which receives the matter of the celestial bodies).

Maimonides, recognising the scientific difficulties of these two accounts of creation in addition to the problems associated with the thesis of the world's eternity, attempts to create a system that will protect the validity of the law no matter what science would ultimately prove. This, however, leads to a series of controversies because in some places Maimonides seems to hold the position of creation *ex nihilo*, whereas in others he seems to presume the world's eternity. In modern Jewish philosophy, creation figures most highly in the thought of **Franz Rosenzweig,** who argues that the term signifies the relationship between God and the world. He claims, much like Plato, that the universe is originally in a state of uniformity, but through divine will it is made diverse.

See **Abravanel, Isaac; afterlife; Albo, Joseph; Aristotelianism; belief; creation a parte ante; creation a parte post; creation, eternal; Cohen, Hermann; Crescas, Hasdai; divine will; eternity; Genesis; Gersonides; God knowledge of; God, nature of; halakhah; immortality; Maimonidean controversies; Maimonides, Moses; matter; miracles; nature; Neoplatonism; prophecy; physics; Platonism; religion; revelation; Rosenzweig, Franz; Saadia Gaon**

Further reading: Brague 2003; Eisen 1995; Frank and Leaman 1997 and 2003; Goodman 1992; Harvey 1998; Hayoun 1986; Kellner 1986; Kraemer 1991; Lawee 2001; Rudavsky 2000; Samuelson 1994; Silver 1965; Twersky 1980

creation a parte ante: This is a term used to refer to the ungenerated nature of the universe. In the work of Aristotle an ungenerated universe necessarily implied an incorruptible one (i.e. that which does not have a beginning cannot have an end). Not all medieval Jewish philosophers agreed: **Gersonides,** for example, argues that the world was generated, but would not cease to exist.

See **creation; creation a parte post; eternity; Gersonides**

creation a parte post: This is a term used to refer to the incorruptible nature of the universe. Although in the work of Aristotle an incorruptible universe necessarily implied an ungenerated one (i.e. that which does not have an end cannot have a beginning), for medieval Jewish philosophers this implication did not necessarily follow.

See **creation; creation a parte ante; eternity**

creation, eternal: This account posits creation as the eternal production of the world. Since God is an efficient cause, he must eternally produce the universe, since it would be absurd for an efficient cause to be idle. This position was popular among Jewish Averroists, such as **Moses Narboni.**

See **Albalag, Isaac; Averroes; creation a parte ante; creation a parte post; eternity; Gersonides; God, nature of; matter; Narboni, Moses**

Crescas, Hasdai (d. 1412) was an important communal leader among the Jews of Saragossa (Spain). In the anti-Jewish riots of 1391 his only son was murdered in Barcelona.

After that much of his life was spent reconstructing the Jewish communities that had been destroyed. He wrote *The Refutation of Christian Dogma* in the Catalan dialect in order to counter the abundant literature aimed at converting Jews to Christianity, and the *Sermon on Passover* (*Derashat ha-Pesach*), which deals with theological matters such as **belief, miracles, prophecy,** and the legal aspects of Passover.

His most important work of philosophy is the *Light of the Lord* (*Or ha-Shem*), written in Hebrew in 1410. The central aim of the work is to undermine the philosophical claims of **Maimonides** by deconstructing the Aristotelian premises on which the Maimonidean system was based. By refuting the scientific foundations of Jewish philosophy, Crescas hopes to convince his contemporaries to renounce Maimonidean rationalism, which he believed led to the spiritual decline of Spanish Jewry. Even though Crescas is an important critic of philosophy, he is also a philosopher of the first order, and many of his ideas would influence Christian thinkers of the sixteenth and seventeenth centuries. For example, Crescas argues that the infinite can exist *in actu*, and that, because God is infinite, there can exist an infinity of space, time and causal series.

On a political level, Crescas is critical of the Maimonidean claim that locates human **happiness** in the knowledge of the intelligible world, rather than in the fear and love of God, which, for Crescas, grows out of the performance of the **commandments**. Such happiness is open to all of Israel, not just the philosophers. For Crescas, **God** is not an intellect thinking itself, but a personal, dynamic and free entity. In response to Maimonides' articulation of the beliefs that a Jew must believe, Crescas argues that individuals cannot choose true beliefs, but rather such beliefs are compelled upon the believer since they are imposed from without.

See **Abner of Burgos**; **Albo, Joseph**; **Aristotelianism**; belief; commandments; divine will; **Gersonides**; God, knowledge of; God, love of; God, nature of; **Halevi, Judah**; happiness; **Maimonidean controversies**; **Maimonides, Moses**; miracles; **Narboni, Moses**; prophecy; religious experience; Scholasticism; theology

Further reading: Frank and Leaman 1997 and 2003; Harvey 1998; Kellner 1986; Kreisel 2001; Sirat 1985; H.A. Wolfson 1957

determinism: The central philosophical question surrounding determinism is whether it is compatible with human freedom. This, in turn, is related to the question of moral responsibility. Can one be punished for an act if it has been predetermined that one will commit that act? This question gains added seriousness in trying to understand tragic moments in Jewish history, for example, in the mass conversion of Jews to Christianity in the fourteenth century, or the **Shoah** in the twentieth century.

See **Abner of Burgos**; **Aristoteliansim**; **Asharites**; astronomy; **compatibilism and incompatibilism**; **Crescas, Hasdai**; divine will; ethics; evil, problem of; history; kalam; **Mutazilites**; omnipotence; omniscience; **Polleqar, Isaac**; providence; **Shoah, the**

Further reading: Leaman 1997

divine attributes: The central philosophical questions that revolve around ascribing attributes to God are ontological, epistemological and linguistic. Ontologically, how are we able to assign attributes to God without jeopardising his unity? If God does possess attributes, in what way can they be said to exist? Epistemologically, how are we able to know that God possesses attributes? And, linguistically, how can we talk about God? When the Bible speaks of God's strength or God's speech, how does it employ such terms? Are they symbols, metaphors or analogies? Most Jewish philosophers stress the absolute unity and unfathomability of the divine essence, while claiming that we can know something of God's attributes of action (e.g. righteousness, loving kindness). **Saadia,** following the Muslim **kalam,** denies the existence of separate divine attributes, and instead insists on the perfect unity of God with his knowledge, wisdom, life, etc.

For medieval Aristotelians, when we say that God is merciful this does not mean that God possesses the trait of mercy, only that we ascribe to God activities that in a human context we associate with mercy. According to **Maimonides,** all of the attributes that we apply to God are 'negative', that is, they are attributes whose opposites are to be negated of God. To say that God possesses life, for example, means that we negate of God the trait of death. In order to read such theories of attribution into the Bible, many medieval philosophers argue that biblical descriptions of God have to be read as if they were **allegory. Hermann Cohen,** developing the medieval discussion of attributes of action, is less concerned with who God is as with what God does. The divine attributes of action become, for him, much like Maimonides, models of human action.

See **allegoresis; allegory; Aristotelianism; Asharites; Cohen, Hermann; emanation; ethics; evil, problem of; God, knowledge of; God, nature of; happiness; kabbalah; kalam; Maimonidean controversies; Maimonides, Moses; metaphor; miracles; Mutazilites; negative theology; providence; religious language; Saadia Gaon**

Further reading: Frank and Leaman 1997; Sirat 1985; H.A. Wolfson 1979

divine will: The will, understood traditionally, is the faculty of choice or decision, by which an individual determines which actions to perform. The divine will, then, is that part or attribute of God responsible for action in the world. However, the system of **emanation**, which was foundational to all medieval Aristotelian and Neoplatonic **cosmology**, tends to preclude any will on the part of God, making God's activity in the world mechanical and based on intermediary forces. Samuel **ibn Tibbon**, for example, probably goes the furthest when he equates God's will with the natural order. **Ibn Gabirol** tries to reintroduce a voluntary aspect back into God by arguing that the divine will, sometimes equated with wisdom, is responsible for creating universal **form** and **matter**. **Judah Halevi** also attempts to retain God's volitional power by dispensing with the entire series of emanated intellects, and replacing it with the *amr* ('logos') so that God can act whenever and however he wants. **Maimonides** argues that the divine will is uncaused and does not act essentially for the sake of anything else; it does, however, desire that optimal existence prevail in all species.

See **angels**; **determinism**; **divine attributes**; **evil, problem of**; **Gersonides**; **God, knowledge of**; **God, nature of**; **Ibn Gabirol, Shlomo**; **ibn Tibbons**; **Maimonidean controversies**; **Maimonides, Moses**; **monotheism**; **omnipotence**; **omniscience**; **providence**

Further reading: Guttmann 1964; Kreisel 2001; Lobel 2000; Sirat 1985

dogma: Traditional Judaism never defined a Jew in terms of beliefs, but as a person born of a Jewish mother or a person converted to Judaism. The encounter with Islam and **Karaism**, however, increasingly forced Jewish thinkers to define Judaism in propositional terms. The true believer was now defined based on his or her assent to certain propositions. Thinkers as diverse as **Saadia Gaon**,

Maimonides, Albo, Crescas and Isaac Abravanel define religious belief not simply as trust or faith, but as the affirmation or denial of certain dogmatic statements (e.g. afterlife, creation, immortality, Mosaic prophecy). Moses Mendelssohn is critical of this approach, and he argues that Judaism possesses no dogma, only divine legislation (e.g. commandments, statutes). This is also the position of Geiger and Baeck, the latter of whom contends that the attempt to make a set of dogmatic statements that every Jew must believe is tantamount to confessionalism.

See Abravanel, Isaac; afterlife; Albo, Joseph; Baeck, Leo; belief; creation; Crescas, Hasdai; Maimonidean controversies; Maimonides, Moses; prophecy

Further reading: Kellner 1986

E

emanation: The central problem that emanation seeks to solve is how multiplicity (i.e. our world of form and matter) emerges from unity (i.e. God). As developed by Alfarabi and Avicenna, the self-reflection or self-intellection of the One entails the emergence of a pure Intellect. By contemplating itself and its source, this pure Intellect gives rise to a second intellect and the outermost sphere of the heavens. The subsequent sequence of intellects and spheres carries down to the tenth and lowest of the supernal or heavenly intellects, the Active Intellect, and the nethermost celestial sphere, that of the moon. This emanative framework continues into the sphere below the moon, with the Active Intellect responsible for the projection of universal forms or archetypes onto matter.

Informed critics of philosophy, such as Judah Halevi and Isaac Abravanel, reject this theory for (1) introducing too many intermediaries between God and the world,

(2) making God's creativity a mechanical process, (3) negating the **divine will** and (4) making the Active Intellect, not God, responsible for the governance of our world. Although Halevi tries to negate the system of emanation, it was the medieval system of **cosmology**; as a result, the best he can do is posit a volitional emanation, which has precedents in **Saadia Gaon** and **ibn Gabirol**. The system of emanation fell out of favour with the emergence of Copernican astronomy.

See **Abravanel, Isaac; Active Intellect; Alexander of Aphrodisias; Alfarabi; angels; astronomy; Avicenna; celestial spheres; cosmology; creation; creation, eternal; divine will; form; Genesis; Halevi, Judah; Ibn Gabirol, Shlomo; Maimonidean controversies; matter; Neoplatonism; Plotinus; Saadia Gaon; Themistius**

Enlightenment: The Enlightenment, perhaps best epitomised by **Immanuel Kant**'s telling phrase, 'Dare to Know', put tremendous emphasis on reason over clerical authority, and universal human rationality over ethnicity. Riding on the back of the Enlightenment was the Jewish Enlightenment (known in Hebrew as the *Haskalah*), which represented the intellectual effort to assess and reform Judaism based on Enlightenment ideals.

One of the earliest and best-known figures of the Jewish Enlightenment is **Moses Mendelssohn**, who argues that Judaism is a rational religion predicated on a rational understanding of God and a historical relationship to him. Israel's relationship to God is not one of doctrine (something that Kant was extremely critical of), but of law. According to him, true Judaism is a revealed legislation based on rational truths and laws.

Subsequent Jewish Enlightenment thinkers, such as **Abraham Geiger**, take Mendelssohn's ideas to their extreme conclusions, arguing that certain parts of the halakhah (e.g. mixing of meat and dairy products) are historical relics and, because they do not fit with reason, can be safely ignored in the modern world. This, not surprisingly, caused a backlash from more observant Jews. Many of the modern denominations of Judaism (e.g. Reform, Orthodox, Conservative) emerge during this period.

See **aesthetics; commandments; Geiger, Abraham; halakhah; Kant, Immanuel; Krochmal, Nachman; Mendelssohn, Moses; reason; Wissenschaft des Judentums**

Further reading: Altmann 1973; Feiner 2002; Frank and Leaman 1997; Harris 1991; Mendes-Flohr and Reinharz 1995; Meyer 1967; Myers 2003; Samuelson 1989; Sorkin 1996

epistemology: A sub-discipline of philosophy that is concerned with the nature, sources and limits of human knowledge. In Jewish philosophy, whether medieval or modern, this must involve the compatibility between natural reason and traditional authority. In medieval epistemology, human knowledge is, for the most part, predicated on some form of relationship between the human intellect and the **Active Intellect**. This often involves the Active Intellect imparting knowledge of forms into the human intellect, culminating in, among certain individuals at least, the state of **prophecy**.

Most epistemology is described as either 'foundationalist' in which an individual is able to progress from basic propositions derived through, for example, observation, to inferred propositions through, for example, deduction or induction. The opposite position is known as 'coherentism,' which denies foundational propositions in favour of a mutual dependence that emerges from a coherent set of beliefs. Modern theories of epistemology tend to be based on the 'foundationalist' model: Empiricists (e.g. Hume) argue that basic beliefs derive from either the senses or introspection; Rationalists (e.g. **Baruch Spinoza**) contend that these basic beliefs derive from rational or a priori intuition; and Innatists (e.g. **Immanuel Kant, Hermann Cohen**) argue that there exist some beliefs that are innate to humans. Post-Modern thought critiques traditional epistemology owing to the subject's inability to declare itself based on various political, historical and cultural contexts.

See **Active Intellect; God, knowledge of; Kant, Immanuel; Levinas, Emmanuel; Moses; Post-Modernism; prophecy**

Further reading: Fakhry 1983; Frank and Leaman 1997 and 2003; Goodman 1992; Gordon 2003; Hayoun 1986; Hughes 2004a; Kreisel 2001; Lobel 2000; Myers 2003; E.R. Wolfson 1994

essence and existence: The difference between essence and existence is associated most closely with the thought of **Avicenna**, even though it seems likely that he derived this distinction from **Alfarabi** or an even earlier source. Essence answers the question, 'what is it?' The answer to such a question must take into account the form or species (e.g. the essence of man is a 'rational bipedal animal'). Existence, in contrast, answers the question, 'does it exist?' Because the intellect can conceive of essences that do not exist in reality (e.g. that of a unicorn), essence and existence are ontologically distinct. Existence, according to Avicenna, is an accident of essence.

See **Active Intellect; Alfarabi; Avicenna; God, arguments for the existence of; God, nature of**

eternity: Much of Aristotelian science, the major scientific system of the Middle Ages, was predicated on the universe being eternal. The problem that this poses for Judaism is probably stated most succinctly by **Maimonides,** who argued that belief in eternity negated the **halakhah,** which is contingent upon God *qua* Creator of the universe. In the post-Maimonidean period, however, a number of thinkers, most notably Samuel **ibn Tibbon** and **Moses Narboni,** tend to radicalise Maimonides, arguing that he really held that the universe was eternal.

The thesis of the eternity of the world and that this is the position of Jewish philosophers, whether or nor they explicitly held it, leads to a series of backlashes against philosophy, which are known as the **Maimonidean controversies.** Most modern Jewish philosophers, when they do take an interest in the debate between creation and eternity, tend to emphasise the former, albeit understood in modern terms (e.g. 'big-bang' theory). For **Franz Rosenzweig,** the concept of eternity has a somewhat different valence. Eternity, he contends, must be foregrounded in temporal existence; he subsequently locates this 'earthly eternity' in the land-less and state-less collective experience of the Jews.

See **Aristotelianism; belief; creation; creation a parte ante; creation a parte post; creation, eternal; cosmology; dogma; Gersonides; halakhah; Ibn Tibbons; Maimonidean controversies; Maimonides, Moses; Narboni, Moses; Rosenzweig, Franz**

Further reading: Eisen 1995; Frank and Leaman 1997 and 2003; Goodman 1992; Hayoun 1986; Kellner 1986; Kraemer 1991; Lawee 2001; Rudavsky 2000; Samuelson 1994; Silver 1965

ethics: That which ascertains the human good in action. Ethics is thus practical because the right thing to do is not fixed, but varies according to different scenarios and sets of circumstances. Central to the medieval understanding of ethics is the thought of Aristotle, who argued that the good that humans seek is the end for the sake of which every act is done. Excellent actions are noble and done for no other reason than that they are noble. Basic to this is the proper balance of all the soul's functions. The attainment of this balance, most Jewish philosophers would argue, comes about through the proper understanding of the precepts enumerated in the **Torah**.

One of the earliest attempts to work out the connection between Torah, virtue and reason is provided by **Philo of Alexandria** who argues that individuals must improve themselves by means of the acquisition of virtues based on the Aristotelian doctrine of the mean (e.g. the mean between cowardice and rashness is bravery). Furthermore, like many of the philosophers who came after him, Philo contends that human reason is not sufficient to ascertain what constituted the good life. What is needed is **revelation**, which is perceived to be in harmony with the laws of **nature**.

If Aristotle was the figure behind much of medieval Jewish philosophical speculation on ethics, the person behind much of modern discussion of ethics is **Immanuel Kant**. According to him, ethics is based not on virtue ethics that puts pride of place on the individual but on duty ascertained through abstract and universal rules. In Jewish philosophy this is seen most clearly in the work of **Hermann Cohen**. Other Jewish thinkers, most notably **Buber** and **Levinas**, link ethics not to speculation but to concrete relationships that the individual self has with other human beings. But whereas Buber would argue that ethics constitutes our response to God, Levinas claims that it is ethics that leads to our experience of God.

See **autonomy; Buber, Martin; Cohen, Hermann; divine attributes; God, knowledge of; God, love of;**

happiness; Kant, Immanuel; Levinas, Emmanuel; nature; Philo of Alexandria; revelation; Shoah, the; Torah

Further reading: Gordon 2003; Kaplan 1996; Kreisel 1999; Samuelson 1989; Seeskin 1990; Tirosh-Samuelson 2003

Existentialism: Existentialism arose as a backlash against philosophical and scientific systems that treated particulars as members of a genus. Existentialists therefore start out with a detailed description of the self as an agent involved in specific social and historical contexts. One of the central aims of Existentialism is to understand how the individual can achieve the richest and most fulfilling life in the modern world. This life is frequently described using the term 'authenticity'.

Martin Buber, for example, emphasises the importance of dialogue between individuals as leading to authenticity. At the heart of his system resides the I–Thou relationship, which is a way of responding to another based on their status as a genuine person. **Joseph Soloveitchik** expresses this in more traditional religious terms when he claims that the Talmudic scholar, or 'halakhic man', represents the archetype of the modern man of action. It is through the **halakhah,** he argues, that an individual finds true human dignity and autonomy. **Mordechai Kaplan,** in contrast, stresses collective as opposed to individual Existentialism; this enables him to preserve the identity, unity and continuity of the **Jewish people** and their religion in the modern world.

See **autonomy; Buber, Martin; ethics; halakhah; Hegel, Georg Wilhelm Friedrich; Heidegger, Martin; historicism; history; Jewish people; Kaplan, Mordechai; Levinas, Emmanuel; Rosenzweig, Franz**

Further reading: Batnitzky 2000; Frank and Leaman 1997; Gordon 2003; Guttman 1964; Leaman 1997; Myers 2003; Samuelson 1989; Seeskin 2001

evil, problem of: The logical problem of evil is that if it exists, and we clearly observe that it does, how does God relate to it? Is he unable to eradicate evil? If so, what does this say about God's omnipotence? The classical Jewish account of the problem of evil is found in the book of Job, wherein an innocent man seems to suffer for no apparent reason. One possible response is that offered by the notion of free will: evil has to exist so that humans can make appropriate choices. The standard medieval philosophical approach to evil was that it was simply a privation of goodness. Death, for example, is the privation of life, not the opposite of it. Evil thus has no independent existence. Maimonides argues that evil is contingent upon matter, not God, and that the good is consequent upon form. The goal of philosophy is to disengage the individual from matter by studying the sciences and thereby perfecting the intellect. A different approach to evil was offered by the kabbalah, which makes evil part of the cosmic unfolding of God in the universe. Evil is now part of a grand cosmic myth in which every kabbalist partakes.

The modern period, especially with horrendous events such as the Shoah that intended to wipe out the Jewish people, is likewise unsatisfied with defining evil simply in terms of privation. According to Buber, God is in eclipse and evil seriously impedes the I–Thou relationship. Emil Fackenheim, another philosopher responding to the Shoah, posits that this event represents a form of evil never before contemplated. The way to respond to it is through resistance, in both thought and action.

See Buber, Martin; covenant; determinism; Fackenheim, Emil; form; free will; God, nature of; kabbalah;

Maimonides, Moses; matter; omnipotence; Shoah, the; theodicy

Further reading: Eisen 2004; Frank and Leaman 1997 and 2003; Goodman 1992; Katz 1992; Leaman 1997; Samuelson 1989; Seeskin 1990

Fackenheim, Emil (1916–2004) was born in Germany, but forced to flee in light of the rise of Nazism. An ordained rabbi, he also completed a doctorate on the role of substance in the **Ikhwan al-Safa'** at the University of Toronto, where he subsequently taught. Later in his life, he migrated to the state of **Israel**. Fackenheim's early thought, best articulated in *The Religious Dimension in Hegel's Thought*, which provides a penetrating exposition and analysis of **Hegel**, was heavily influenced by German **Idealism**. In particular, Fackenheim is interested in the human–divine encounter and how this encounter is central to the religious life.

In 1966 he increasingly turns his attention to making sense of **the Shoah**, trying to fathom the depths of the **problem of evil** and its subsequent repercussions on reason and faith. His famous conclusion, articulated in works such as *The Human Condition after Auschwitz* and *God's Presence in History*, is that God was present at Auschwitz and that his 'voice' spoke to Jews, telling them that they must resist Nazi atrocities and continue to do so in order not to grant Hitler a posthumous victory. In his *To Mend the World*, Fackenheim focuses on the importance of action, as opposed to just thought, which he was beginning to regard as inadequate on its own. Thus, influenced by **Existentialism**, Fackenheim's thought, taken as a whole, stresses the importance of lived experience, and the interconnections between philosophy and **theology**, thought and action, ideas and history.

See **anti-Semitism; Buber, Martin; Existentialism; evil, problem of; God, nature of; Hegel, Georg Wilhelm Friedrich; history; Idealism; Ikhwan al-Safa'; Israel, state of; Jewish people; Shoah, the; Zionism**

Further reading: Katz 1992; Leaman 1997; Samuelson 1989; Seeskin 1990

Ficino, Marsilio (1433–99) was a Florentine philosopher, translator and theologian. He was also interested in music, magic, medicine, astrology, demonology and other occult sciences. Ficino was largely responsible for the Renaissance revival of Plato; he was also profoundly influenced by the **rational mysticism** of **Plotinus**, which was based on the **immortality** of the **soul**. Ficino is considered the founder of *prisca theologica*, 'ancient theology', which he articulated in his *Platonic Theology*. The theory of 'ancient theology' posits that there exists one universal truth, in which various schools of thought participate. Ancient pagan thinkers – for example, Plato, Zoroaster, Hermes Trismegistus, Orpheus and Pythagoras – all represent different dimensions of an underlying universal truth. Ficino and his contemporaries (especially **Pico della Mirandola**) fitted Judaism, in particular **kabbalah**, into this theological system, thereby acknowledging Judaism as a true religion, something that was rarely done by Christian thinkers prior to this. In addition to his translations of Plato and Plotinus, Ficino also wrote the *Commentary on Plato's Symposium*, which inaugurated the genre of philosophical treatments of love, a genre that would quickly include the *Dialoghi d'amore* of **Judah Abravanel**.

See **Abravanel, Judah; immortality; kabbalah; Neopla-tonism; Pico della Mirandola, Giovanni; Platonism; Plotinus; rational mysticism**

form: Form, unlike **matter,** is what is intelligible to the human intellect. According to the ancient and medieval philosophers, we know that Saul is a human not because of the matter from which he is composed but because he belongs to the form, or species, of humanness. In other words, form is that which makes one species distinct from other species. The form of the human species, according to most medieval philosophers, is the rational capacity of the intellect. The concept of form is also basic to medieval **cosmology,** which posits a sharp distinction between the celestial (extending from the outermost orb to that of the moon) and terrestrial (the earth and its atmosphere) worlds. Both worlds contain bodies made of matter and form, both of which are in constant motion. But only the terrestrial world undergoes change owing to the extreme fluctuating character of its matter. Change occurs in the terrestrial world because bodies undergo growth, diminution, generation and corruption since matter constantly exchanges one form for another.

See **Aristotelianism; cosmology; creation; essence and existence; evil, problem of; God, knowledge of; Maimonides, Moses; matter; Neoplatonism; Platonism**

free will: Free will implies that we have the power to perform a specific action (e.g. going to the synagogue this Friday night) or to refrain from performing it (e.g. not going to the synagogue this Friday night). The concept of free will is the opposite of that of determinism, both of which revolve around the notion of God's foreknowledge. If I go or do not go to the synagogue this Friday night, does God have foreknowledge that I will or will not perform this act? If he does, then I do not have the free will to choose for myself; if he does not, then God's **omniscience** is called into question.

Virtually all of the Jewish philosophers make room for our free will in their systems. For example, if **God** is pure intellect, then an intellect cannot know particulars, but only universals; in which case, God is unconcerned with whether or not I go to the synagogue this Friday night. Less radical is the position (e.g. **Maimonides**) that claims that I have no idea whether God knows that I will go to the synagogue this Friday night, but that I have to work on the assumption that I do in fact have the free will to choose whether or not I will go.

See **Abner of Burgos; astrology; compatiblism and incompatibilism; determinism; divine will; Gersonides; God, nature of; kalam; omnipotence; omniscience; providence**

Further reading: Eisen 2004; Feldman 2003; Frank and Leaman 1997 and 2003; Katz 1992; Leaman 1997

Geiger, Abraham (1810–74) was a historian, philosopher, theologian and the intellectual founder of Reform Judaism. Obtaining rabbinic ordination, in addition to a doctorate in Oriental Studies, Geiger was part of a generation of Jewish thinkers interested in creating the foundations for a new Judaism, one that was pleasing in terms of **aesthetics** and that fitted with modern German sensibilities. These German-Jewish reformers looked back romantically at the great medieval philosophers, especially **ibn Gabirol** and **Maimonides**, as their own intellectual precursors who also struggled to bring the Jews of their day from superstition to informed worship.

In his *Judaism and Its History*, Geiger attempts to show how, using an evolutionary framework, the rabbinic period was one of aridity and that, because of this, the normative sources of Judaism could be revised since they did not constitute the essence of the tradition. This led to a rethinking of the role and meaning of the **covenant** and the **halakhah** in modern Jewish life. Needless to say, this caused a tremendous backlash among other thinkers, who argued that Geiger was trying to dismantle Judaism. This can be witnessed in the various feuds that erupted in congregations and cities in which Geiger served as rabbi.

See **aesthetics; commandments; covenant; Enlightenment; halakhah; Hirsch, Samson Raphael; history; Ibn Gabirol, Shlomo; Jewish people; Kaplan, Mordechai; Maimonides, Moses; Mendelssohn, Moses; Rosenzweig, Franz; Wissenschaft des Judentums**

Further reading: Frank and Leaman 1997; Mendes-Flohr and Reinharz 1995; Meyer 1967; Myers 2003

Genesis: When Jewish philosophers usually refer to the book of Genesis, they are most interested in the first few chapters that discuss the account of **creation**, in Hebrew known as *ma'aseh bereshit*. Other important topics that received philosophical consideration in this book include the **covenant** between God and all future generations of the **Jewish people** through Abraham. The book of Genesis has been a staple of Jewish philosophical speculation from **Philo** of Alexandria to the present.

See **Abravanel, Isaac; chosenness; covenant; creation; creation a parte ante; creation a parte post; creation, eternal; Gersonides; God, arguments for the existence of; Noahide laws; religious language; Rosenzweig, Franz; Torah**

gentiles: That gentiles, or non-Jews, are distinct from Jews is basic to Jewish self-understanding. But what exactly constitutes the difference? In formulating responses to this question, Jewish thinkers have historically answered it by claiming that gentiles differ from Jews either ontologically (i.e. their very being), theologically (i.e. their belief systems) or metaphysically (i.e. their creation or soul). A related problem concerns the relationship between the learned or philosophical gentile (e.g. Aristotle or **Alfarabi**) and the ignorant Jew. Because medieval philosophers equate religious perfection with intellectual perfection, the non-Jewish philosopher obviously has to have a place in the world to come, whereas the Jewish ignoramus cannot be guaranteed such a position. Moreover, if **prophecy** is regarded as a natural phenomenon, then ostensibly anyone, Jew or gentile, with the requisite intellectual perfections could attain it. Indeed, this is **Maimonides**' position, at least in his *Epistle to Yemen*.

In response to such universalising tendencies, particularistic thinkers, such as **Judah Halevi**, argue that only the **Jewish people** have an intimate relationship with God. Even the convert to Judaism, according to Halevi, is on a lower ontological level than the native-born Jew. If we label Maimonides' position with regard to gentiles 'universalistic' and Halevi's 'particularistic', we see these two positions continuing into the modern period. The universalistic approach is clearly discernible in the writings of **Buber** and **Cohen**, who interpret concepts such as Israel's **chosenness** in terms of universal categories (e.g. the Jew's mission to all of humanity); the more particularistic approach can be found in the work of **Rosenzweig**, who argues that the Jewish people enjoy an ontological priority over all other communities, because they alone have a proper orientation towards the future, an orientation that does not involve idols such as statehood.

See **chosenness**; **Cohen, Hermann**; **covenant**; **Halevi, Judah**; **Hebrew**; **Jewish people**; **Maimonidean** controversies; Maimonides, Moses; Noahide laws; prophecy; Rosenzweig, Franz; Zionism

Further reading: Eisen 1995; Kellner 1991; Myers 2003

Gersonides (1288–1344), also known by his acronym Ralbag, was one of the most important Jewish philosophers of the medieval period. His writings include biblical commentaries, super-commentaries on **Averroes'** commentaries to Aristotle, his original philosophical treatise known as *The Wars of the Lord* (*Milhamot ha-Shem*), in addition to numerous mathematical and astronomical treatises. After his death, prominent individuals such as **Hasdai Crescas** and **Isaac Abravanel** criticised his writings for their unorthodox quality.

His biblical commentaries, most of which were written after the *Wars*, provide probing philosophical analyses of key texts, showing how the Bible illumines discussions of the **commandments**, moral and **political philosophy**, and theoretical sciences such as **physics** and **metaphysics**. Like **Maimonides**, Gersonides perceives the Torah to be the perfect law, and when read properly it alone reveals the true nature of human **happiness**.

It is really in the *Wars*, though, that Gersonides struggles with the twin legacies of **Maimonides** and **Averroes**. Roughly 40 per cent of the *Wars* is concerned with the problem of **creation**; Gersonides believes that the creation of the universe out of pre-existent matter is (1) stated in **Genesis**, (2) provable and (3) that he has proved it, based on such arguments as the absurdity of infinite past time. On the topic of **miracles**, Gersonides rejects the thesis that God can do anything or that he is the direct cause of miracles. For example, he argues that the splitting of the Sea of Reeds was the result of a strong East wind; or that the transformation of Moses' staff into a snake represented the speeding-up of natural laws. The natural process of decomposition and transformation is thus the true 'miracle', and, for Gersonides, the true cause of such miracles is not God, but the **Active Intellect**.

Another important feature of Gersonides' thought is his discussion of **providence**, which he bifurcates into general and individual. General providence is the outcome of God's self-intellection and is responsible for the preservation of all the species in the terrestrial realm. Individual providence, in contrast, is defined as a function of intellectual perfection and, therefore, only attainable by select individuals. This latter type of providence can be inherited from generation to generation.

See **Abravanel, Isaac; Active Intellect; astronomy; Averroes; creation; creation a parte ante; creation a parte post; Genesis; happiness; Maimonidean controversies; Maimonides, Moses; miracles; prophecy; providence; Torah**

Further reading: Eisen 1995; Frank and Leaman 1997 and 2003; Guttmann 1964; Kreisel 2001; Leaman 1997; Sirat 1985; Tirosh-Samuelson 2003

God, arguments for the existence of: Arguments for the existence of God date at least to the time of Aristotle, who argued that there must be a first mover, itself unmoved. The three main arguments in the medieval period for God's existence are cosmological, teleological and ontological. All three are, in various forms, still used today. Cosmological arguments begin from general but a posteriori facts about the universe (e.g. the existence of contingent beings).

In its classical form, the cosmological argument runs as follows: all that moves is moved by something else; there cannot be an infinite series of moved and moving things; therefore, there must exist a first unmoved mover. Jewish philosophers who used versions of this argument include most of the Neoplatonists, **Maimonides** and **Moses Mendelssohn**.

Teleological arguments are based on the fact that the universe has been designed by a conscious and intelligent being. The classic version is: the universe looks as if it has been designed, and the only real candidate for this must be God.

Ontological arguments are based on the absurdity that would follow from positing God's non-existence. The classical form that the ontological argument takes is: God is by definition that being than which none greater can be conceived; that which exists is greater than that which does not exist; if God did not exist, then a being greater than God could be conceived, which is absurd. Versions of the ontological argument were used by, among others, **Gersonides** and Moses Mendelssohn.

See **Aristotelianism; atomism; creation; emanation; Gersonides; God, nature of; kalam; logic; Maimonides, Moses; Mendelssohn, Moses; metaphysics; Neoplatonism; reason**

God, knowledge of: Most Jewish philosophers are in agreement that the highest human good is knowledge of God. Yet, the question remains: how do we attain such knowledge? According to certain thinkers in the rabbinic tradition, this knowledge is attainable through the performance of the **commandments**. Most philosophers agree, but interpret the meaning of the commandments in different ways. Moreover, since most philosophers work on the assumption that God's **essence** is unknowable, the only recourse is through knowledge of the **divine attributes**, especially those of action. For many, knowledge of God is attainable through study of the sciences and intellectual contemplation. This is where the relationship between the microcosm and the macrocosm comes into play: knowledge of the physical world leads to knowledge of the metaphysical world.

Yet, many also connect the knowledge of God to the realm of **ethics**. In the last chapter of the *Guide*, for example, **Maimonides** claims that knowledge of God is tantamount to knowledge of God's action. Consequently, knowledge of God leads to activity in the social or political realms. In modern Jewish philosophy this relationship between knowledge of God and ethics becomes central. In the thought of **Cohen**, for example, God is the archetype of morality; as such, we must imitate God in reaching out to others, just as he reaches out to us as a moral agent. For **Buber**, and even more extremely in **Levinas**, our knowledge of God is likewise dependent upon the relationship we have with the others with whom we come into contact.

See **autonomy; Buber, Martin; Cohen, Hermann; commandments; cosmology; divine attributes; epistemology; essence and existence; ethics; God, nature of; halakhah; kabbalah; Levinas, Emmanuel; Maimonides, Moses; metaphysics; nature; physics; Spinoza, Baruch; Torah**

Further reading: Brague 2003; Hughes 2004a; Idel 1989; Kaplan 1996; Kraemer 1991; Lobel 2000; E.R. Wolfson 1994

God, love of: All of the Jewish philosophers are in agreement that the ideal relationship with God was predicated on love as opposed to fear. Where they differed, however, was what constituted love. For **Maimonides** and other Jewish Aristotelians, love of God is tantamount to **knowledge of God**, which is attainable through intellectual contemplation. Juxtaposed against this view was the one offered by informed critics of philosophy, such as **Judah Halevi** and **Hasdai Crescas**, who locate the love of God in the observance of the **commandments**.

Probably the most sustained treatment of love as a cosmic principle is the work of **Judah Abravanel**, especially his concept of the 'circle of love'. According to this principle, one half of this circle stretches from God to prime matter and is characterised by a paternal love wherein that which is more beautiful desires the perfection of that which is less beautiful. The second half of the circle goes in the other direction and is the love of the inferior to unite with the superior.

In the thought of **Spinoza** (which may have been influenced by Abravanel's discussion), after identifying **God** with nature, he claims that the highest human perfection is the intellectual love of God (*amore Dei intellectualis*), which presumably is based on knowledge of individual things. In modern Jewish philosophy, the love of God also figures highly with individuals connecting it to concepts such as **autonomy** (e.g. **Hermann Cohen**) and personal relations among specific individuals (e.g. **Buber**).

See **Abravanel, Judah; autonomy; Buber, Martin; Cohen, Hermann; commandments; Crescas, Hasdai; Existentialism; God, knowledge of; God, nature of; Halevi, Judah; happiness; Ibn Pakuda, Bachya; Maimonides, Moses; pantheism; rational mysticism; religious experience; Spinoza, Baruch**

Further reading: Hughes 2004a and 2004b; Idel 1989; Lobel 2000; Smith 2003; E.R. Wolfson 1994

God, nature of: Medieval philosophers tend to equate God with intellect. The classic formulation, based on Aristotle, is that of an Intellect thinking Itself. A contested issue in medieval Aristotelian **cosmology**, however, is whether God is the First Intellect or an Intellect that existed beyond the series of emanated intellects. In the Renaissance period, Jewish thinkers, under the increasing influence of the **kabbalah**, begin to develop more **pantheistic** notions of God, culminating in **Spinoza**'s radical concept of 'God or Nature' (*Deus sive Natura*), in which God and **nature**

are one and the same. Unlike his medieval precursors, Spinoza makes God an immanent as opposed to a transcendent force. Some modern philosophers (e.g. **Cohen, Buber**) tend to locate the nature of God in the moral order, whereas others (e.g. **Rosenzweig**) discern this nature in the dynamic interactions between him on the one hand and the world and humanity (especially the Jews) on the other.

See **Aristotelianism; Asharites; Buber, Martin; celestial spheres; creation; Cohen, Hermann; cosmology; divine attributes; emanation; intellect; kabbalah; metaphysics; nature; negative theology; pantheism; Spinoza, Baruch; Rosenzweig, Franz**

Guttmann, Julius (1880–1950) was born in Hildesheim, educated in the tradition of **Wissenschaft des Judentums,** received a PhD in philosophy from the University of Breslau, and in 1935 was appointed Professor of Jewish philosophy at the Hebrew University in Jerusalem. A student of **Hermann Cohen,** Guttmann was both a philosopher and a historian of philosophy. His most famous work is *The Philosophies of Judaism* (*Die Philosophie des Judentums*), which argues that 'Jewish philosophy' is a process by which individuals absorbed foreign ideas to 'elucidate and justify' Judaism as an essential category. At the same time, however, Guttmann is extremely critical of many of the medieval Jewish philosophers, especially **Maimonides,** for their radicalism in subverting traditional or authentic Jewish belief. Guttmann, at least according to the criticisms of **Leo Strauss,** understands Jewish philosophy as an aspect of culture and thus failed to understand how Jewish (and Islamic) philosophers grounded religion in divine laws. Guttmann responds to this critique by defending his own textual-historical approach for appreciating the categories of medieval philosophy in all of their contextual complexities and criticising Strauss's method for, among other things, importing modern concerns into the medieval data, and unduly bifurcating faith and reason. Guttmann also wrote on the concept of God in **Kant**, and, more generally on the philosophy of religion.

See **Aristotelianism; Cohen, Hermann; Kant, Immanuel; Maimonidean controversies; Maimonides, Moses; Strauss, Leo; Wissenschaft des Judentums; Zionism**

Further reading: Green 1993; Guttmann 1964

halakhah, or Jewish law that is derived from the divine **commandments**, establishes, according to rabbinic theology, the relationship between God and Israel. One of the central philosophical questions surrounding the halakhah is whether it is a means to an end or an end in and of itself. If the goal of philosophy is the **happiness** that results from intellectual perfection, then how do the laws of Judaism, especially the more arcane ones (e.g. not mixing meat or dairy, or not mixing mules and oxen when plowing one's field), contribute to the telos of human life? In order to minimise the tension between these two domains, the majority of medieval philosophers attempt to show the rational basis of the halakhah. When this cannot be done, they are often content to claim that it contributes to the welfare of the body (e.g. circumcision dulls the sexual appetite).

In modern Jewish philosophy the status of halakhah is perhaps best summarised in the debate between **Buber** and **Rosenzweig**. According to the former, strict observance of the law is potentially dangerous because it focuses on legislation as opposed to the dialogue that one should have with God that derives from the personal and living interactions with others; according to the latter, however, strict adherence to the law is what enables the Jew to take an active role in creating and sustaining meaning in the world.

See **commandments; Crescas, Hasdai; God, knowledge of; Halevi, Judah; happiness; Jewish people; Karaites; Moses; political philosophy; Rosenzweig, Franz; Soloveitchik, Joseph; Torah**

Further reading: Eisen 1995; Harris 1991; Kellner 1986 and 1991; Samuelson 1989; Seeskin 2001; Twersky 1980

Halevi, Judah (1075–1141) was one of the most important secular and religious poets of al-Andalus. At the age of fifty, he renounced Andalusi culture as inauthentic, and set sail for the land of Israel. To show his opposition to the Jewish-Arabic synthesis of the Middle Ages and the dangers it posed for Jews, Halevi wrote his *Kuzari*, one of the most important and popular books of Jewish thought. This work established Halevi as one of the most sustained and informed critics of philosophy. (He is often compared to **Alghazali**, who offered similar informed criticisms of Islamic philosophy.)

For Halevi, religion has to be grounded in a subjective and personal experience not rational explanation. The proof for this is to be found in **history** and the historical record, not philosophy. He is thus critical of the standard philosophical arguments that God could not have created the world from nothing or has no knowledge of particulars. Halevi instead emphasises the particularism of the Jewish tradition (unlike **Maimonides**, who highlights Judaism's universalism). Despite this it is important not to read Halevi simply as an anti-rationalist. This is too easy; for, on one level, Halevi works within a philosophical framework (e.g. he is critical of simplistic anthropomorphism and spends considerable time on the **divine attributes**). He is most critical of philosophy when it comes to the philosophers' equation of **divine will** with **nature**, their denial that God can intervene directly in the world, and their naturalisation of **prophecy**. What Halevi does is make proper action and deeds (as understood according to the **halakhah**) superior to rational speculation. In his claim that religion must permeate one's whole being and that the Jewish people are ontologically different from other nations, Halevi's thought would influence a number of later thinkers, including **Franz Rosenzweig** (who translated Halevi's poetry into German).

See **Abravanel, Isaac; Active Intellect; Aristotelianism; commandments; creation; Crescas, Hasdai; divine attributes; divine will; God, knowledge of; halakhah; history; Jewish people; miracles; prophecy; religious experience; Rosenzweig, Franz**

Further reading: Frank and Leaman 1997 and 2003; Guttmann 1964; Lobel 2000; Sirat 1985; Tanenbaum 2002; E.R. Wolfson 1994

happiness, as understood by philosophy, means flourishing and experiencing well-being that is appropriate to human beings. The single most important influence on medieval philosophical speculation on happiness was Aristotle, especially his *Nicomachean Ethics*. For Aristotle, happiness (or *eudaimonia*) was not equivalent to contentment or joy, but was tantamount to a stable pattern of living, which he equated with the life of intellectual contemplation. The only way to reach such a state of living, however, was to develop a moral personality that curbed desires and cultivated virtues through the doctrine of the mean. This is often referred to as virtue **ethics** or ethics of virtue.

In Judaism, however, this discussion of happiness also had to take into account the notion of the **Torah**, which establishes and defines the relationship between God and the **Jewish people**. Accordingly most Jewish philosophers locate their discourse of happiness as human flourishing in the pattern of life established by the Torah, which is historically interpreted in different ways. The Torah, for example, is what establishes a regimen for human well-being by acknowledging that humans are comprised of body and soul, and providing the means of perfecting both.

Yet, because philosophers tend to equate happiness with knowledge, the question arises: what knowledge leads to happiness? Rationalists claim that such knowledge could only come from the philosophical sciences, whereas those critical of philosophy argue that human happiness cannot be found in 'foreign' wisdom, but in the **halakhah** alone. Increasingly in the modern world, Aristotle's notion of virtue ethics has been replaced by the ethics of duty, especially as formulated by **Kant**, and interpreted for Judaism by thinkers such as **Hermann Cohen**.

See **autonomy; Cohen, Hermann; commandments; covenant; ethics; halakhah; Jewish people; Kant, Immanuel; Maimonidean controversies; political philosophy**

Further reading: Seeskin 2001; Tirosh-Samuelson 2003

Hebrew: Although Hebrew was not a spoken language from biblical times until the present, many works of Jewish philosophy tended to be written in Hebrew. Perhaps two notable historical exceptions are Muslim Spain and nineteenth- and twentieth-century Germany, where there already existed highly sophisticated and long-established languages of philosophy, Arabic and German respectively. In Spain, many works were written in Judeo-Arabic

(Arabic in Hebrew characters). Such works include **Saadia**'s *Book of Beliefs and Opinions*, **Bachya ibn Pakuda**'s *Duties of the Heart*, **Maimonides**' *Guide of the Perplexed* and **Judah Halevi**'s *Kuzari* (which is an interesting example since, as one of the greatest cases for Jewish particularism, it was written in Arabic, although this was undoubtedly to appeal to as broad a Jewish audience as possible). In Germany, many works of Jewish philosophy were written in German; examples being **Cohen**'s *Religion of Reason out of the Sources of Judaism*, **Buber**'s *I and Thou* and **Rosenzweig**'s *Star of Redemption*. One of the earliest works of Jewish philosophy written in Hebrew was **Abraham bar Hiyya**'s *Meditation of the Sad Soul*. The tendency in Jewish philosophy is to regard Hebrew as a conventional language. This is the opposite of the mystical approach to Hebrew, which tends to regard Hebrew as an ontological system, with the Hebrew letters functioning as the building blocks of creation.

See **Abulafia, Abraham; bar Hiyya, Abraham; Buber, Martin; Cohen, Hermann; Enlightenment; Halevi, Judah; Ibn Pakuda, Bachya; kabbalah; Rosenzweig, Franz; Saadia Gaon**

Hegel, Georg Wilhelm Friedrich (1770–1831) was one of the last of the German Idealists, whose thought represents a reaction against **Immanuel Kant**. For Hegel, Kant failed to provide a unified theory of reality, something he himself tried to do in his highly influential *Phenomenology of Spirit*. For Hegel, world history is the development of spirit (*Geist*) and freedom (*Freiheit*) that progresses dialectically. Beginning in the 'Orient', it moves to Greece and then culminates in the European-Protestant culture of his own day. In terms of his philosophy of religion, Hegel is interested not only in God but also in the way that God appears in the religious consciousness. For Hegel, this is found most perfectly in Protestant Christianity, which is able to mediate the opposition between the finite and infinite through the Trinity. He is also extremely critical of **Judaism**, accusing its conception of God as being too abstract and far-removed from the world, thus instilling in Jews a sense of fear and self-negation. Despite this critical attitude, Hegel would have a tremendous influence on contemporaneous and later Jewish thinkers (e.g. **Nachman Krochmal**). However, he was criticised by neo-Kantians such as **Hermann Cohen**.

See **commandments; covenant; Cohen, Hermann; Enlightenment; God, nature of; Heidegger, Martin; history; Idealism; Jewish people; Krochmal, Nachman; Mendelssohn, Moses; Rosenzweig, Franz**

Further reading: Gordon 2003; Harris 1991; Mack 2003

Heidegger, Martin (1889–1976) is the most important philosopher of the twentieth century. His impact on Jewish philosophy, however, has been problematic owing to his support for the Nazis and his dismissal of Jews, including his mentor Edmund Husserl, from teaching positions at Freiburg University. His influential *Being and Time* (*Sein und Zeit*) would have a tremendous influence on many fields of modern philosophy, from Existentialism to **hermeneutics** to deconstruction, in addition to cognate disciplines such as literary criticism.

For Heidegger, we are 'thrown into' a world of limited sense that is constantly shaped by our own deaths. Meaning or significance, therefore, is always finite or phenomenal. Much of his work is concerned with uncovering the nature of being, especially the being of humans (what he calls *Dasein*). *Dasein* is temporal in the sense that it is always becoming. The meaning of any entity is nothing more than how that entity is understood by human experience (i.e. in time). Since being can only be disclosed temporally and finitely, we only understand being discursively and partially, but never essentially. His post-Second World War thought is extremely obscure, and in it he seems to favour a rich and contemplative poetic thinking instead of the exactitude of phenomenology. A major critic of Heidegger was **Leo Strauss**, who argued that his use of **history** was misleading, that his thought led to atheism and the subsequent abnegation of divine law, or truth, and nihilism. Related to this critique, others have argued that his association with Nazism was not simply a form of careerism, but was intimately connected to his phenomenology.

See **anti-Semitism; hermeneutics; historicism; history; Post-Modernism; Strauss, Leo**

Further reading: Batnitzky 2000; Gordon 2003; Green 1993

hermeneutics: One could quite easily make the case that Judaism is predicated on hermeneutics, or the art of interpretation, especially when it comes to the biblical narrative. Jewish philosophy is also hermeneutical, with Jewish philosophers engaged in a project of interpreting the biblical and rabbinic texts according to various models of rationality inherited from the larger culture in which they found themselves (e.g. Platonic in the case of **Philo**, Aristotelian in the case of **Maimonides**, Kantian in the case of **Cohen**). The concept of hermeneutics is also related to Maimonides' *Guide of the Perplexed* which was written in such a manner that later (medieval and modern) commentators interpret Maimonides as saying different things depending on their own philosophical agendas (e.g. the controversy over **creation**). In the contemporary period, one can speak of 'traditional' hermeneutics, 'feminist' hermeneutics, 'post-modern' hermeneutics, etc., all of which bring different interpretive strategies often to the same text or set of texts.

See **allegoresis**; **allegory**; **Cohen, Hermann**; **creation**; **halakhah**; **Heidegger, Martin**; **Maimonidean controversies**; **Philo of Alexandria**; **Plaskow, Judith**; **Post-Modernism**

Heschel, Abraham Joshua (1907–72) was born in Warsaw, received his PhD at the University of Berlin, and then moved to the United States in 1940, where he taught at Hebrew Union College in Cincinnati and then at the Jewish Theological Seminary in New York. Unlike most of the medieval philosophers who defined God as an intellect and, thus, impassive to human concerns, Heschel argues that the God of the Bible was a passionate God, who cared deeply for the world, as evinced by **prophecy**. In *The Sabbath*, Heschel claims, in part influenced by the phenomenology of **Heidegger**, that the Sabbath provides an oasis from what is otherwise the technologising of the week and, by extension, the world.

Heschel is perhaps best known for *God in Search of Man: A Philosophy of Judaism*, wherein he argues that the central focus of Judaism is the **halakhah** because it is what enables the **Jewish people** to engage in a relationship with God by responding to his **transcendence**. God, in turn, desires a relationship with the world as is witnessed in the **history** of the Jewish people, and through the **commandments** God reaches out to the Jews. Perhaps influenced by the Conservative movement within Judaism (the Jewish Theological Seminary being the centre of this movement), Heschel claims, contra certain strands of Orthodoxy, that the divine commandments are not ends in themselves, but a human response to God; and, contra the Reform movement, the commandments cannot be replaced by mere sentiment.

See **Buber, Martin; commandments; covenant; God, love of; halakhah; Heidegger, Martin; Jewish people; prophecy; transcendence; Wissenschaft des Judentums**
Further reading: Kaplan 1996

Hirsch, Samson Raphael (1808–88) was the chief rabbi at Oldenburg and the chief defender of Orthodoxy in Germany in the light of Reform critiques. In *Horeb*, Hirsch sets out to explain the reasons for the **commandments,** his idea being that a proper understanding of the commandments would automatically lead into the performance of them. Although orthodox, Hirsch is by no means opposed to philosophy or the ideals of the **Enlightenment**. In order to show the compatibility between Judaism and modernity, Hirsch interprets the former through a Kantian prism. For instance, he argues that transcendent **metaphysics** and any sort of speculative theology are impossible, and that human knowledge is confined solely to the practical or moral sphere. But whereas **Kant** equated morality with **autonomy** and 'self-legislation', Hirsch stresses the centrality of practical **revelation**. In *The Religious Philosophy of the Jews*, Hirsch claims that the Jews have made a central and important contribution to human civilisation. Here he is critical of thinkers such as Kant and **Hegel,** both of whom claimed that Christianity had surpassed Judaism.

See **autonomy; Cohen, Hermann; commandments; Enlightenment; ethics; Geiger, Abraham; God, knowledge of; Jewish people; Kant, Immanuel; metaphysics; revelation; Torah; Wissenschaft des Judentums**
Further reading: Frank and Leaman 1997

historicism: A term employed by late eighteenth- and nineteenth-century thinkers to restore individuality to historical processes. Each historical event was unique, developed through its own internal mechanisms and had to be understood within its own particular context. Historicism was, thus, opposed to the contemporaneous tendency to understand history according to the theoretical claims of philosophy, which regarded historical events as part of the unfolding of a transcendent natural law. Jewish historicism, then, is the absorption of the ideals and vocabulary of historicism to understand Jewish history on its own terms, as an interconnected series of individual events, personalities, etc. It is perhaps best associated with the movement known as **Wissenschaft des Judentums**, which attempts to justify Judaism on scientific principles. The philosophical problem that historicism gives rise to is: if Judaism is simply the sum of interconnected historical forces, how does one understand the uniqueness of the **Jewish people**?

See **aesthetics; Enlightenment; Geiger, Abraham; Guttmann, Julius; history; Ibn Kaspi, Joseph; Idealism; Jewish people; Krochmal, Nachman; Mendelssohn, Moses; Spinoza, Baruch; Wissenschaft des Judentums**
Further reading: Gordon 2003; Myers 2003

history: Philosophy is notoriously unconcerned with history. Whereas philosophy is all about the eternal and the unchanging, history is about particular individuals making specific choices that have important repercussions. In the medieval period, history was not a university discipline governed by social scientific principles as it is today, but was conceived as a spiritual drama in which a particular group of people saw itself as the primary actors. In traditional Judaism, for example, history is understood as a three-pronged process consisting of **creation, revelation** and **redemption**; it is through the historical record (e.g. the Exodus from Egypt) that God established his **covenant** with the **Jewish people**. This is why more conservative thinkers, such as **Halevi,** argue that religious experience is to be witnessed in history not philosophy.

In the modern period, with the rise of **Wissenschaft des Judentums,** many Jewish philosophers regard history, now defined and excavated according to social scientific principles, as essential to Jewish self-understanding. One attempt to mitigate the potential relativism that history posed for Judaism is offered by **Samson Raphael Hirsch** who claims that Judaism has no history (Jews might have a history, but Judaism does not); another is proposed by **Franz Rosenzweig** who argues that the **Jewish people** exist on a supra-historical level, and are thus not subject to the ebb and flow of history in the same manner that other peoples are.

See **chosenness; covenant; creation; Enlightenment; Halevi, Judah; historicism; Ibn Daud, Abraham; Ibn Kaspi, Joseph; Jewish people; Kaplan, Mordechai; Krochmal, Nachman; revelation; Rosenzweig, Franz; Spinoza, Baruch; Wissenschaft des Judentums; Zionism**

Further reading: Frank and Leaman 1997; Harris 1991; Myers 2003

human perfection *see* **happiness**

Ibn Bajja (d. 1138) was a Muslim philosopher who lived in al-Andalus. He wrote a paraphrase of Aristotle's *Physics*, a number of glosses on **Alfarabi's** logical works and two original treatises, *The Governance of the Solitary* (*Tadbir al-Mutawahhid*) and the *Epistle on Conjunction* (*Risāla al-ittisāl*). The former work is primarily concerned with the best political regime for the philosophical life. Like Alfarabi, he lists what the ideal state consists of, in addition to enumerating various corrupt regimes. His central claim is that if a philosopher cannot find an ideal state in which to live, it is incumbent upon him to live alone, either literally (i.e. in the countryside) or figuratively in a larger society. Ibn Bajja further divides human actions into those that are voluntary and involuntary, the latter arising from impulse and the former from rational choice. Only humans are capable of voluntary actions. Yet he argues that the actions of the citizens of corrupt states are involuntary, essentially equating them with animals. Following **Alexander of Aphrodisias**, ibn Bajja defines the intellect as a disposition to cognise intelligibles, and that which survives corporeal death is the actualised intellect. In his *Epistle on Conjunction*, ibn Bajja argues that the goal of the philosophical life is conjunction (*ittisāl*) with the **Active Intellect**. Ibn Bajja's work would influence Jewish thinkers such as **Maimonides**. **Moses Narboni** translated the *Governance of the Solitary* into **Hebrew** and wrote a commentary to it in the fourteenth century.

See **Active Intellect; Alexander of Aphrodisias; Alfarabi; happiness; Maimonides, Moses; Narboni, Moses; political philosophy; rational mysticism; Themistius**

Further reading: Fakhry 1983; Leaman and Nasr 1996

Ibn Daud, Abraham (c. 1110–c. 80) was born in Muslim Spain, subsequently fled to Christian Spain where he died as a martyr for unknown reasons. He wrote a work of **history**, known as *The Book of Tradition* (*Sefer ha-Kabbalah*), which details the history of the Jews from biblical times to his own day, and stresses, against the claims of the **Karaites**, the centrality of rabbinic leadership to authentic Jewish life. Philosophically, ibn Daud's *Exalted Faith* (*Ha-Emunah ha-Ramah*), written in Arabic but survives only in **Hebrew** translation, represents the first systematic effort by a Jewish philosopher to engage and apply the new science associated with **Aristotelianism**. The work itself is divided into three books: the first introduces Aristotelian terms and concepts (e.g. substance, the ten categories, motion); the second establishes six basic principles of Judaism (e.g. God is a necessary being, God is one, centrality of the **Torah, prophecy**) and interprets them in light of Chapter 1; and the third deals with ethics.

A problem that preoccupies ibn Daud, and in the introduction he gives it as his reason for writing the work, is the problem of **free will** and **determinism**. He deals with this in his sixth principle of Book 2, and argues that choice is essential because God punishes disobedience. How could he punish it, if humans had no choice in the matter? His solution is that God, as omniscient and omnipotent, determines everything, yet humans still have choice. The key here is that the Bible must be read properly so that terms predicated of God should not be understood literally but equivocally. Ibn Daud, as the first Jewish Aristotelian, would exert considerable influence on subsequent thinkers such as **Maimonides** and **Gersonides**: Of particular importance was his claim that true religion and philosophy are not incompatible, but should be coherent in the quest for **truth**.

See **allegoresis; Aristotelianism; Avicenna; Gersonides; God, nature of; history; Karaites; Maimonides, Moses; omnipotence; omniscience; prophecy; religious language; Torah**

Further reading: Frank and Leaman 1997; Guttmann 1964; Sirat 1985

Ibn Ezra, Abraham (1089–1140) was a poet, philosopher, scientist and biblical exegete. Born in Muslim Spain, he spent most of the later years of his life travelling throughout

Europe, disseminating the ideals and sciences associated with Jewish learning in Muslim Spain to other Jewish communities in Italy and Northern Europe. His biblical commentaries, still published in rabbinic Bibles, provide a wealth of philosophical information, although much of this philosophical material is scattered here and there, giving rise to the notion that ibn Ezra was an unsystematic thinker. His most philosophical treatise is *Yesod Mora*, a work whose goal is to explain the **commandments**, and the interrelationship between Judaism and the various sciences. Ibn Ezra also translated many scientific treatises into Hebrew, thus functioning as an important figure in the domestication of Islamic sciences in Judaism.

Ibn Ezra seems to have been the first Jewish philosopher to employ **Avicenna**'s important distinction between necessary and contingent existence. Otherwise, he is a fairly standard Neoplatonist, who upheld **emanation,** the idea that the human soul is part of the universal soul, and if the individual properly takes care of it (i.e. by following the **commandments** and studying the sciences), it will return to its celestial home upon the death of the body. Ibn Ezra is also very fond of **astrology,** interpreting many of the biblical events (e.g. the Golden Calf) in terms of astrological principles and astral magic.

Ibn Ezra's commentaries to the Bible would become very popular in the fourteenth century because they presented an alternative to what was often perceived to be the extreme rationalism of Maimonides. This gave rise to a number of supercommentaries (e.g. of **ibn Kaspi**), or commentaries on the commentary of ibn Ezra.

See **astrology; Avicenna; commandments; commentary; emanation; Ibn Kaspi, Joseph; Karaites; Neoplatonism; rational mysticism; Torah**

Further reading: Hughes 2004a; Sirat 1985; E.R. Wolfson 1994

Ibn Falaquera, Shem Tov (c. 1225–c. 1295) was a poet and philosopher who lived in Provence. He did not claim to be a particularly original philosopher, and many of his works consisted of Arabic extracts translated into Hebrew. Among the works he translated into Hebrew were the *Book of Five Substances* by Pseudo-Empedocles and parts of the *Fountain of Life* (*Meqor ha-Hayyim*) by **ibn Gabirol**. He is known primarily for the compilation of encyclopediae, a genre whose primary goal was systemisation and organisation as opposed to originality. His two best-known encyclopediae are *The Beginning of Knowledge* (*Reshit ha-Hokhmah*) and *The Book of the Seeker* (*Sefer ha-Mevakesh*). These works were responsible for the dissemination of Aristotelian and Maimonidean principles to a larger Hebrew readership. He also wrote the *Guide to the Guide*, an explication of certain passages of **Maimonides'** *magnum opus*, which was used by subsequent commentators.

See **Aristotelianism; commentary; Ibn Gabirol, Shlomo; Maimonidean controversies**

Further reading: Frank and Leaman 1997 and 2003; Sirat 1985

Ibn Gabirol, Shlomo (1021–c. 58) was one of the great Jewish poets of Muslim Spain; he composed both religious and secular poetry, in addition to being one of the most original of the Jewish Neoplatonists. His most famous philosophical work, the *Fountain of Life* (*Meqor ha-Hayyim*), written in Arabic, was translated into Latin and known as the *Fons Vitae*, where it had considerable influence on scholastic thinkers. Many of the themes in the *Fountain of Life*, for example, emanation, the fate of the human soul, microcosm–macrocosm, can also be found in poetic form in his *Kingly Crown* (*Keter Malkut*). He also wrote a treatise called *The Improvement of the Moral Qualities*

(*Tikkun Middot ha-Nefesh*), which describes the various qualities of the soul, emphasising the Aristotelian doctrine of the mean.

In the *Fountain of Life*, ibn Gabirol, as a good Neoplatonist, claims that knowledge of oneself (i.e. the microcosm) leads to knowledge of the universe (i.e. the macrocosm); that knowledge is the true goal of human life; and that such knowledge will enable the soul to reascend to its heavenly home upon the death of the body. Ibn Gabirol is a monist, who argues that **matter** and **form** exist on every level of reality, including the intelligible world. Matter, as potentiality, and form, functioning as the process of individualisation, both come from God. Ibn Gabirol is also interested in the principle of **divine will**. The Neoplatonic system of emanation left little room for any will on the part of God. Ibn Gabirol attempts to get around this by reintroducing God's Will as the force that puts together universal form and universal matter, whose combination creates, in order, the divine Intellect, the divine Soul, **nature** and simple substances. Ibn Gabirol thereby ascribes to God a voluntary aspect.

See **divine will; emanation; ethics; form; God, nature of; happiness; Ibn Tibbons; matter; Neoplatonism; nature**

Further reading: Frank and Leaman 1997 and 2003; Guttmann 1964; Sirat 1985

Ibn Kaspi, Joseph (1279–c. 1332) wrote **commentaries** on the Bible, **Maimonides'** *Guide of the Perplexed* and **ibn Ezra**'s biblical commentaries. Writing at the height of the **Maimonidean controversies**, ibn Kaspi was part of a group of thinkers responsible for the radicalisation of Maimonidean principles. Ibn Kaspi claims, among other things, that the proper way to understand the Bible was through the knowledge supplied by disciplines such as logic, grammar and **history**. This, he argues, would lead to a 'natural' and literal understanding of the text. Ibn Kaspi is, therefore, opposed to the idea that the masses be taught only the exoteric meaning of the text. In terms of history, ibn Kaspi makes the innovative claim that the Bible is a historical book that reflects the spatial and temporal milieux in which it was composed. This radical (for its time) **historicism** calls into question a number of the supernatural events of the Bible (e.g. **prophecy, miracles**). In this regard, some see ibn Kaspi as a precursor to **Spinoza**.

See **Averroes; commentary; hermeneutics; historicism; history; Ibn Tibbons; Maimonidean controversies; miracles; Narboni, Moses; Spinoza, Baruch; Torah**

Further reading: Herring 1982; Sirat 1985

Ibn Pakuda, Bachya (second half of eleventh century) was a judge in Saragossa (Muslim Spain) where he also wrote his major philosophical-mystical work *Duties of the Heart* (*Hidaya ila Fara'id al-Qulub*). It was translated into **Hebrew** as *Hovot ha-Levavot* by Judah **ibn Tibbon** and quickly became one of the most popular works among subsequent Jewish pietists.

Influenced by Muslim mystics, or Sufis, the main tenor of Bachya's work is to awaken in Jews the duties of the heart (inner experience) as opposed to simply duties of the limb (outer expression) that are performed perfunctorily. These duties of the heart, while rational, are judged only by God. Bachya divides his treatise into ten chapters, the structure of which follows closely that of works written by Muslim mystics. Philosophically, the thought of Bachya is most influenced by **kalam** thinkers (e.g. nothing can create itself, therefore there must be a creator; since unity precedes plurality, one creator must have created the universe). He also employs **Neoplatonic** ideas in his discussion of God's unity: only unity, being and eternity are essential attributes of God. None of these, however, implies any sort of plurality in God's essence, but only a denial of their opposites. Like the **Mutazilites**, Bachya argues that scriptural anthropomorphisms used to describe God must be understood metaphorically.

See **Asharites; cosmology; divine attributes; God, arguments for the existence of; God, love of; God, nature of; Halevi, Judah; kabbalah; metaphor; Mutazilites; prayer; rational mysticism; religious experience; soul**

Further reading: Frank and Leaman 1997 and 2003; Guttmann 1964; Sirat 1985; Tirosh-Samuelson 2003

Ibn **Tibbons** were a family of translators, responsible for translating many works of philosophy written in Arabic (by both Muslims and Jews) into **Hebrew**. They are of significance because they were responsible for introducing philosophical ideas to generations of Jews who no longer read Arabic, thus disseminating and popularising the ideas of Judeo-Islamic philosophy to the Jewish communities of Southern France and beyond. Judah ibn Tibbon (1120–90) was responsible for translating some of the classics of Jewish philosophy into Hebrew: **Saadia Gaon**'s *Book of Beliefs and Opinions*, **ibn Gabirol**'s *The Improvement of the Moral Qualities*, **Halevi**'s *Kuzari* and **Bachya**'s *Duties of the Heart*.

Judah's son, Samuel (d. c. 1232), translated works of Aristotle and Galen, in addition to **Maimonides**' *Guide of the Perplexed*. He also wrote his own works, including a commentary on Qoheleth, and *Let the Waters Be Gathered* (*Ma'amar Yikkawu ha-Mayyim*), a commentary of Genesis 1: 9 based on the Aristotelian principle of the four elements (earth, air, fire and water). Samuel's commentaries, thus, take Maimonidean principles and apply them directly to the biblical narrative.

Samuel argued, contrary to Maimonides, that average Jews should be taught the philosophical secrets hidden in the **Torah**. This would play an important role in the subsequent **Maimonidean controversies**. Judah's son, Moses ibn Tibbon (d. after 1283), was also a prodigious translator, translating works by Aristotle, **Themistius** and **Averroes**. His original philosophical works were written as commentaries (e.g. to the Bible, to **ibn Ezra**'s commentaries).

See **allegoresis; allegory; commentary; Genesis; Ibn Pakuda, Bachya; Maimonidean controversies**

Further reading: Frank and Leaman 1997 and 2003; Guttmann 1964; Sirat 1985

Ibn Tufayl (d. 1185) was an important Islamic philosopher who lived in al-Andalus. Only one work of his survives, *Living, Son of Awake* (*Hayy ibn Yaqzan*), a philosophical **allegory** describing the life of the soul according to the doctrines of **Neoplatonism** and **rational mysticism**. The treatise itself describes the intellectual development of its protagonist in completely natural terms: as the protagonist observes the patterns and unity behind natural phenomena, he proceeds from the physical and biological sciences to the astronomical sciences until he reaches the supreme science of **metaphysics**. By observing the multiplicity of the natural world, the protagonist gradually realises that there must exist a unified, incorporeal principle that acts as its causal agent. This leads him to prove the existence of God.

Following the protagonist's rational mystical relationship with God, ibn Tufayl switches the focus of the narrative to the realm of **political philosophy**, that is, the best state in which an individual can find **happiness**. As the result of his adventures with other people, the protagonist quickly becomes aware that most are unable to fathom the true nature of God, and that they prefer to think of him in simplistic and anthropomorphic terms. He nonetheless realises that religion plays an important political function because it establishes social harmony. *Hayy ibn Yaqzan* exerted influence on subsequent Jewish philosophy. The *Chapter on Beatitude*, a text attributed to Maimonides, favourably cites ibn Tufayl's work. *Hayy ibn Yaqzan* was eventually translated into Hebrew and commented on by **Moses Narboni**, whereupon it became a staple of the philosophical curriculum of late medieval and renaissance Jews.

See **allegory; cosmology; emanation; God, arguments for the existence of; God, love of; happiness; metaphysics; Narboni, Moses; Neoplatonism; political philosophy; rational mysticism; religious experience**

Further reading: Fakhry 1983; Hayoun 1986; Hughes 2004a; Leaman and Nasr 1996

Ibn Zaddik (d. 1149) was a poet and philosopher belonging to the important circle of thinkers that included **Judah Halevi** and **Abraham ibn Ezra**. His main philosophical work is the *Microcosm* (*ha-Olam ha-katan*), which was written in Arabic, but survives only in Hebrew translation. As the name of this treatise suggests, ibn Zaddik argues that knowledge of the human body leads to knowledge of the physical world, and knowledge of the human soul leads to knowledge of the intelligible world. Knowledge of entities is derived from two sources, the senses and the intellect. The senses provide knowledge of the physical things (e.g. accidental qualities) and the intellect allows the individual to apprehend essences. The latter knowledge in particular allows humans to understand God's attributes of action (which can only be understood metaphorically), but not his essence. Ibn Zaddik also seems to equate philosophy with **prophecy**:

Whereas the ancient Israelites had prophecy, subsequent generations of Jews have to learn the same truths through science.

Although ibn Zaddik was almost alone among the medieval Neoplatonists in arguing for **creation** ex nihilo (here he relies heavily on the arguments of the **Mutazilites**), his theory of the human soul is the standard Neoplatonic one: vegetative, animal and rational souls, only the last of which is immortal, but which must be properly cultivated through the study of philosophy so that it can ascend to its celestial home after the death of the body. Reward and punishment will be meted out not in this world but in the celestial world (e.g. the souls of the wicked will not return to the universal Soul, but will be caught in the constant motion of the heavenly spheres, which are associated with fire). Like **Saadia**, he divides the **commandments** into those of reason (e.g. prohibition against murder) and those of revelation (e.g. not mixing meat and dairy).

See **afterlife; commandments; cosmology; creation; divine attributes; emanation; God, knowledge of; God, nature of; Halevi, Judah; happiness; Ibn Ezra, Abraham; negative theology; Neoplatonism; prophecy; Saadia Gaon; soul; theodicy**

Further reading: Frank and Leaman 1997 and 2003, Guttmann 1964, Sirat 1985

Idealism: Defined by the notion that the human mind exists as the most basic reality and that the world exists as an appearance to the mind. It is often associated with the thought of **Immanuel Kant,** and his desire to derive the principles of knowledge and ethics from the **autonomy** of the human intellect. Central to Idealism is the difference and distinctiveness of Judaism, and how it was regarded as a religion that was inferior to Protestant Christianity, which was perceived by the likes of Kant and **Hegel** to be the epitome of human civilisation because of its ability to integrate the finite with the infinite.

One of the earliest Jewish responses to this is offered by **Nachman Krochmal**, who argues that the principles of Idealism existed in early Jewish texts, which describe God as the unity of all existence (thereby mediating the finite–infinite antinomy that was so bothersome to Kant and Hegel). **Rosenzweig**, with his 'New Thinking', offers an alternative to Idealism, a philosophy based on **revelation** and the hermeneutic of religious experience that is existentially grounded in community, language and ritual.

See **anti-Semitism; Buber, Martin; Cohen, Hermann; Enlightenment; Hegel, Georg Wilhelm Friedrich; Krochmal, Nachman; revelation; Rosenzweig, Franz; Zionism**

Further reading: Batnitzky 2000; Gordon 2003; Mack 2003; Samuelson 1989

Ikhwan al-Safa', or the 'Brethren of Puruty', were a ninth-century philosophical brotherhood from Iraq that was associated with Ismaili circles. They formed a philosophical secret society that stressed initiation, the renunciation of the world and its trappings, and the quest for philosophical truth and gnosis. They and those associated with them are responsible for fifty-two epistles (*rasa'īl*) that circulated widely throughout the Muslim world. Influenced by **Neopythagoreanism**, they stress the centrality of mathematics and numbers for a proper understanding of the universe (macrocosm) and the individual (microcosm), and the way they relate to one another. Just as God is the first principle of the universe, the number one is the first principle of numbers. This number symbolism enables them to connect various phenomena (e.g. four elements = four humours = four primary qualities = four seasons = four corners of a square; twelve bodily orifices correspond to the twelve signs of the zodiac).

Their psychology is essentially that of **Neoplatonism**, stressing the soul's imprisonment in the body and its subsequent desire to return to its celestial home. Their physics is derived from Aristotelian principles (e.g. **form, matter,** motion). The teachings of the Brethren, thus, represent the eclectic intellectual milieu of the tenth century, in which Platonic, Aristotelian, Neopythagorean and Neoplatonic doctrines intersected. The Epistles were introduced into Muslim Spain in the early eleventh century by al-Kirmani, a contemporary of **ibn Gabirol,** who also lived in Saragossa. Influences of the Brethren can be detected in virtually all of the Andalusi Jewish philosophers who subscribed to Neoplatonism.

See **Aristotelianism;** astrology; **Baghdad; emanation; God, knowledge of; God, nature of; Halevi, Judah; Ibn Ezra, Abraham; Ibn Gabirol, Shlomo; Neoplatonism; Neopythagoreanism; Plotinus; Theology of Aristotle**

Further reading: Fakhry 1983; Hughes 2004a; Leaman and Nasr 1996

imagination: If one is told to imagine a yellow flower, one can do this easily even if there is no yellow flower present. This ability to make present that which is absent has traditionally led many philosophers to mistrust the imagination. Plato, for example, denigrates the imagination for its ability to create things that are either not present or have no existence in reality (e.g. a unicorn). He juxtaposes the imagination with the **intellect,** the faculty responsible for discerning intelligibles. Despite this, Plato never hesitates from asking his reader to call to mind some principle, which is itself a work of the imagination. On one level, most medieval philosophers tend to agree with Plato; however, on another level, they need the imagination because many, especially those influenced by **Neoplatonism**, equate the goals of their philosophical systems with an imaginative vision of the divine presence. Aristotelians, such as **Maimonides**, are generally more mistrustful of the imagination, yet they still give this faculty a central role in their theories of **prophecy**. For them, the imagination is that faculty which enables the prophet, qua perfect philosopher, to receive and coin images that will be able to appeal to those who are not trained in philosophy. Indeed, Maimonides defines prophecy as an overflow from the **Active Intellect** into the prophet's intellect and then his imagination. Even though he will argue that the imagination played no role in **Moses**' prophetic career, Maimonides still has to admit that Moses needed his imagination to communicate to the masses.

Spinoza in this instance, as in so many others, stands traditional Jewish philosophy on its head and argues that prophets are known for their rather vivid imaginations at the expense of their intellects. In modern philosophy, **Immanuel Kant** argues in his first critique that the imagination is common to both practical and theoretical reason and, because of this, becomes a primary medium for thought. This led many subsequent thinkers, Jewish and non-Jewish, to stress the important role of poetry and the imagination in philosophy. **Franz Rosenzweig**, for example, contends that poetry is the original form of understanding, something that he tries to replicate in the highly literary quality of his *Star of Redemption*, and something that he and **Martin Buber** attempt to reveal in their own German translation of the Bible.

See **Active Intellect; cosmology; Gersonides; God, knowledge of; happiness; intellect; Maimonides, Moses; metaphysics; Moses; Neoplatonism; Plotinus; prophecy;**

rational mysticism; religious experience; Rosenzweig, Franz; Spinoza, Baruch

Further reading: Batnitzky 2000; Hughes 2004a and 2004b; Kreisel 1999 and 2001; Lobel 2000; Tanenbaum 2002; E.R. Wolfson 1994

immortality: Jewish philosophers generally consider immortality, or the concept of eternal existence, as the goal of human life. Virtually all of these thinkers agree that there exists some part of the individual, that which constitutes the essence of humans *qua* humans, that survives the death of the body. This essence is most often defined as the **intellect** or the rational **soul**. Whereas traditional Judaism and more conservative thinkers would argue immortality is derived through the proper relationship that the individual has with God through the observance of the **commandments,** the philosophers tend to locate immortality in the acquisition and mastery of secular sciences.

Philo and most of the medieval thinkers argue that humans are a composite of body and soul, two substances that unite for the duration of one's life. The goal of life is to care for the soul so that it will become Godlike. This is what will enable the soul to attain everlasting life. Those influenced by **Aristotelianism** talk more about the intellect than the soul: human immortality now consists primarily in the conjunction between the human intellect and the **Active Intellect**. There is a certain amount of disagreement as to whether or not immortality is personal or impersonal. Most seem to contend that immortality is impersonal since only the perfected intellect can become immortal, with corporeal aspects of individuals departing with the death of the body. **Gersonides**, however, following **Alexander of Aphrodisias**, argues that the intellect is not a substance, but only the ability to cognise. As a result, he contends that immortality occurs not through conjunction with a divine intellect, but through the individual knowledge that each individual acquires in his or her life.

According to **Moses Mendelssohn,** the immortality of the soul is based on the notion that God is good and, because of this, our world is the best of all possible worlds. Therefore, one's soul would not only continue to exist but also it would continue to exist as one's own soul. **Franz Rosenzweig** says that immortality, which he associates with redemption, is a condition that applies to a community not an individual; it is only through collective experiences, for example, those of ritual, that unite the past, present and future that permit a community to live beyond the meanings associated with the world.

See **afterlife; Alexander of Aphrodisias; Aristotelianism; commandments; emanation; Gersonides; happiness; intellect; Mendelssohn, Moses; Neoplatonism; soul**

Further reading: Harvey 1998; Hayoun 1986; Kraemer 1991; Kreisel 1999 and 2001; Reines 1970

intellect: The medieval philosophers use the term intellect in a number of ways. First, the intellect is regarded by most philosophers to be the essence of the individual, the faculty that humans do not share with any of the other animals. Here there are two different theories of the intellect. Those who follow **Alexander of Aphrodisias** argue that the intellect is a disposition to cognise, whereas those who follow **Themistius** claim that the intellect is a substance. Jewish thinkers, following their Muslim contemporaries, tend to differentiate between the potential intellect, that is, the potential to cognise intelligibles (or forms), the active intellect, that is, the human intellect that begins to acquire knowledge, and the acquired intellect, that is, the intellect that is able to think itself and is thus independent of the body.

Second, the divine or celestial world is composed of a number of emanated intellects that emerge (often non-temporally) from God or the First Intellect thinking itself and that terminates in the tenth Intellect, known as the **Active Intellect**. During the act of human intellection either the Active Intellect emanates forms (e.g. a triangle as a three-sided entity with 180 degrees) into the human intellect (this was the position of **Avicenna**) or the human intellect abstracts **form** from **matter** through the 'light' of the Active Intellect (this was the position of **Alfarabi**).

See **Active Intellect; Alexander of Aphrodisias; Alfarabi; Avicenna; emanation; form; God, nature of; happiness; Maimonides, Moses; matter; prophecy; rational mysticism; soul**

Israel, state of: Although Israel, *qua* the **Jewish people**, has been a perennial issue of Jewish philosophy, the modern geo-political state of Israel is of fairly modern provenance corresponding to the period immediately preceding Israel's foundation (1948) and afterwards. The nature of the state of Israel in Jewish philosophy can perhaps be witnessed most vividly in the contrasting ideas of **Franz Rosenzweig** and **Martin Buber**. Whereas Rosenzweig argues that the Jews are an eternal people existing beyond **history** and therefore in no need of a geographic country or state, Buber claims that the Jews should become a holy people in their own land.

In the aftermath of the **Shoah** and the formation of the state of Israel, the main philosophical question has not been whether Jews should have a homeland, but how to understand the nature and logistics of the state. Is, for example, Israel a state for the Jews or a Jewish state? Some thinkers in Israel, for example, **Yeshayahu Leibowitz**, contend that only in Israel can Jews function as an autonomous political community. Other thinkers, especially those living in the diaspora, argue that Judaism should not be defined in geopolitical terms, but in terms that are civilisational and natural. This is the opinion of **Mordechai Kaplan**, but even he has to concede that the state of Israel would strengthen the Jewish people at a time when they were at their weakest.

See **anti-Semitism; Buber, Martin; history; Jewish people; Kaplan, Mordechai; Leibowitz, Yeshayahu; Rosenzweig, Franz; Shoah, the; Zionism**

Further reading: Frank and Leaman 1997; Friedman 2002; Katz 1992; Mendes-Flohr and Reinharz 1995; Myers 2003

Israeli, Isaac (850–c. 932) was essentially the first thinker after **Philo** to employ philosophical ideas taken directly from Greek sources in order to elucidate Judaism. He was thus the first medieval Jewish philosopher. He wrote many treatises, but his two best-known works are the *Book of Substances* and the *Book of Definitions*. Israeli's cosmology is that of the Neoplatonists, although he contends that God created the first three hypostases (**Intellect**, first **form** and first **matter**) and that from these everything else emanates. Interestingly, though, Israeli introduces the hypostases of matter and form prior to Intellect, something that is found neither in **Plotinus** nor the **Theology of Aristotle**.

As far as the human soul is concerned, Israeli is typical of the Neoplatonists: he differentiates between vegetative, animal and rational souls. The latter is what allows the individual to distinguish between good and evil. As such, it must turn away from the passions of the body, and be illumined through the various sciences so that it can cleave to the divine world. Israeli also develops a theory of **prophecy** in which the prophet grasps reality not through the physical senses, but through spiritual forms that God gives to the prophet so that he can communicate to the people. Israeli did not have a great deal of influence on subsequent Jewish thinkers.

See **creation; emanation; intellect; Neoplatonism; Philo of Alexandria; Plotinus; prophecy; Saadia Gaon; Theology of Aristotle**

Further reading: Frank and Leaman 1997; Guttmann 1964; Sirat 1985

J

Jewish people: The concept of the Jewish people is, not surprisingly, central to both Judaism and Jewish philosophy. That Jews and non-Jews are distinct is a central component of Judaism, although what constitutes this difference is a matter of some debate. As far as Jewish philosophy is concerned, although **Alfarabi** and **Maimonides** (or **Alghazali** and **Halevi**) may share the same **cosmology, epistemology** and prophetology, Alfarabi, as a Muslim, obviously has no interest in the Jewish people whereas Maimonides, a Jew, does.

The central debate concerning the Jewish people, in philosophy as well as theology, is whether Jews possess a unique metaphysical or ontological essence, or whether they possess only a distinct religious heritage. Whereas 'particularists' such as Judah Halevi contend that Jews occupy a more superior level of being than non-Jews (including proselytes to Judaism), 'universalists' such as Maimonides argue that the difference between Jews and non-Jews is only a matter of belief or theology. The particularist thus holds that only Jews benefit from divine **providence, revelation,** and that only Jews can attain **happiness,** whereas the universalist would subscribe to none of these positions.

The status of the Jewish people also plays a large role in modern Jewish philosophy. **Franz Rosenzweig,** adopting the particularist model, argues that Judaism and the Jewish people exist on a superior, ahistorical, level to other religions and peoples. Whereas other thinkers, perhaps most notably **Mordechai Kaplan,** stress the civilisational aspects of the Jewish people as constitutive of their distinctiveness.

See **anti-Semitism; apologetics; commandments; covenant; dogma; halakhah; Halevi, Judah; history; Israel, state of; kabbalah; Kaplan, Mordechai; Maimonides, Moses; prophecy; Rosenzweig, Franz; Sinai; Torah; Zionism**

Further reading: Eisen 1995; Kellner 1991

Judaism see **commandments; covenant; Jewish people**

kabbalah: As one incarnation of Jewish mysticism, kabbalah's emergence is most often associated with the *Zohar* attributed to Moses de Leon in the last half of the thirteenth century. Although influenced by **Neoplatonism,** especially the notion of **emanation,** the kabbalah essentially provides an alternative to the rationalism of philosophy, which kabbalists perceive to be a deviation from authentic Jewish tradition.

Whereas Jewish philosophers argue that the knowledge of God's essence is impossible, the kabbalists claim not only that it is not but also that they actually know it. In so doing, kabbalists create an elaborate myth that involves God, the **Jewish people** and the **Torah.** In particular, God and Israel are involved in a loving (including sexual) relationship that is centred in the Torah. Israel is not something that is distinct from God, but is actually part of God's inner rhythm. As a result, what humans, particularly Jews, do in this world affects God.

The kabbalistic notion of God then is one that is ever changing, not immutable (as it is for the philosophers). The Jewish people are responsible for perfecting God through the performance of the **commandments**, accompanied by the proper intention. The *Zohar* also presents an elaborate discussion of the **problem of evil**. Evil is now regarded as part of a cosmic myth, in which God and the domain of evil ('the other side') are engaged in a perennial struggle. It is also a struggle that the Jewish people are intimately involved in through their observance or lack thereof of the commandments. Kabbalah would, in the sixteenth century, provide both an intellectual and a cultural alternative to rationalism.

See **Abravanel, Judah; Abulafia, Abraham; Alemanno, Yohanan; commandments; emanation; evil, problem of; God, nature of; halakhah; Hebrew; Maimonidean controversies; Messer Leon, David ben Judah; Nahmanides; Neoplatonism; Torah**

Further reading: Frank and Leaman 1997; Scholem 1974; Tirosh-Samuelson 2003; E.R. Wolfson 1994

kalam: The Arabic word that denotes systematic theology (practitioners of kalam are known as *mutakallimun*). It arose because of (1) various theological and political debates in early Islam (e.g. the status of the 'grave sinner', the nature of **free will**) and (2) the desire on the part of certain thinkers to defend the principles of Islam rationally in light of debates with Christian theologians. One of the earliest schools of kalam, the **Mutazilites**, stressed the following five principles: God's justice, unity, his immutable threats and rewards, his commanding right and prohibiting wrong, and the intermediate position of the 'grave sinner' (i.e. between belief and infidelity). They also acknowledged the importance of free will, and the inherent ability of humans to choose between right and wrong. The Mutazilites were also famous for their denial of the eternity of the Koran something they felt infringed on God's unity.

Their main opponents, known as the **Asharites**, argued that God is the only agent in the world and that he directly intervenes in the affairs of the world, and that whatever God commands (even if it goes against reason) is right because whatever he commands must be by definition correct.

Both the Mutazilites and the Asharites divided the **divine attributes** into those of essence (e.g. knowledge, life, power) and those of action (e.g. speech, will, justice). The Asharites would eventually win out and their positions would become orthodox in Sunni Islam. Despite this, Asharism would make virtually no impact on Jewish thinkers. Mutazilism, however, did, and in this respect we can talk about 'Jewish kalam', whose most famous proponent was **Saadia Gaon**, who formulated many of his attacks against the **Karaites** based on the methodology and principles of the Mutazilites.

See **Alghazali; Asharites; atomism; divine attributes; divine will; Karaites; Mutazilites; Saadia Gaon**

Further reading: Fakhry 1983; Frank and Leaman 1997 and 2003; Pines 1997; Sirat 1985

Kant, Immanuel (1724–1804) is one of the most important philosophers of the modern period. He stresses the importance of human **autonomy**, that is, through our use of reason we can both discover and live up to the principles of knowledge without the need of divine revelation. In his *Critique of Pure Reason*, Kant argues that human reason derives knowledge of space and time based on human sensibility, yet such reason can have no knowledge of metaphysics or God. In his *Critique of Practical Reason*, he defines religion as 'the recognition of all duties as divine commands'. Religion is, thus, the provenance of morality and duty.

Kant is, however, notoriously critical of Judaism, describing it as a religion of empty legalism because it is based on statutes devoid of any religious content. For him, a religion that is focused only on a particular people, as opposed to all of humanity, cannot fulfill the basic dictates of morality. Despite Kant's criticism of Judaism, it was not long before Jewish thinkers would begin to formulate an understanding of Judaism using Kantian vocabulary and categories (e.g. **Nachman Krochmal, Hermann Cohen**).

See **anti-Semitism; autonomy; Cohen, Hermann; commandments; Enlightenment; God, knowledge of; Hirsch, Samson Raphael; Krochmal, Nachman; Mendelssohn, Moses**

Further reading: Gordon 2003; Harris 1991; Mack 2003; Samuelson 1989; Seeskin 2001

Kaplan, Mordechai (1881–1983) was a major figure in American Jewish thought, and played a large role in the development of Judaism in America after the Second World War. In his most important work, *Judaism as a Civilization*, Kaplan argues that Judaism is the evolving religious civilisation of the Jewish people. The rise of modern sciences including **history**, Kaplan contends, have brought into serious question the nature of a supernatural God, **miracles, prophecy**, Jewish **chosenness**, etc. This crisis in modern Judaism, especially in the aftermath of the **Shoah,** led to Kaplan's frustration with the various forms of Judaism. For example, he faults both Reform and Orthodox Judaism for making Judaism into a religion of confession. He is also critical of **Zionism** for not paying sufficient attention to the religious dimensions of Judaism. In the place of all of these interpretations of Judaism, Kaplan seeks to create a Judaism that integrated all of the various religious, cultural, sociological and intellectual trajectories of Jewish civilisation. This new 'reconstructed' Judaism has as its central focus the **Jewish people** as opposed to any a priori essence (e.g. God, **covenant**). For it is the Jewish people who, through their evolution, were and are ultimately responsible for the various forms, rites, beliefs, etc. of Judaism.

See **history; Israel, state of; Jewish people**
Further reading: Samuelson 1989

Karaites: A Jewish sectarian movement that acknowledged the validity of the written **Torah**, but denied the authority of the oral Torah. This put them at odds with the Rabbinates (i.e. those who acknowledged both the written and oral Torahs). For Karaites, the true meaning of scripture must emerge from the use of reason as opposed to a chain of tradition. Early Karaites were heavily influenced by theological developments among the Muslim **Mutazilites**; as such they were interested in matters of divine unity (e.g. God's existence and attributes) and justice (e.g. **free will**, reward and punishment). Karaites must have enjoyed considerable popularity because some of the most important Jewish thinkers of the early Middle Ages spent a lot of time refuting them (e.g. **Saadia Gaon, Abraham ibn Ezra, Judah Halevi, Abraham ibn Daud**). Although their popularity quickly waned, there still exist communities of Karaites to this day.

See **Asharites; atomism; determinism; free will; Ibn Daud, Abraham; kalam; Saadia Gaon; Talmud; Torah**
Further reading: Sirat 1985

Kook, Rav (1864–1935) was born in Latvia to a very devout family, but nevertheless studied philosophy. He migrated to Israel in 1904 and became the rabbi of Jaffa. Although he himself was a traditionalist, he nevertheless welcomed the mass migration of secular Jews who, influenced by **Zionism,** were migrating to the land of Israel at this time. Such secular Jews were often criticised by the conservative religious establishment for their secular approach to Judaism and their unwillingness to wait for the Messiah to return the Jews to Israel. Rav Kook, however, argues (influenced by the thought of **Judah Halevi**) that all of the **Jewish people,** no matter what their degree of religious observance, are one people. He is one of the first religious leaders to endorse Zionism, although he is ultimately opposed to what he considered to be the lack of religious commitment among such Jews.

See **chosenness; covenant; Halevi, Judah; Israel, state of; Jewish people; Messianic era; Torah; Zionism**

Krochmal, Nachman (1785–1840) was born and lived in Galicia. The Jewish **Enlightenment,** especially the ideals of **Wissenschaft des Judentums,** influenced him, yet he was not as radical or as political as proponents of this method were in Germany. He mastered the works of both the (medieval and modern) Jewish philosophers, in addition to the thought of modern German philosophy (e.g. **Kant, Hegel,** Schelling). He is particularly fond of **Abraham ibn Ezra,** and frequently reads in his works a precursor to the ideas of Kant and Hegel. This allows Krochmal to argue that Judaism does possess an adequate response to Hegel's critique that Judaism's concept of God was too abstract and remote.

Krochmal's work, the unfinished *Guide of the Perplexed for the Time* (*Moreh Nevukhim ha-Zeman*), is obviously a play on the philosophical *magnum opus* of **Maimonides.** Implicit in this title is the notion that the thought of Maimonides could no longer adequately address the religious needs of contemporary Jews, presumably because the scientific/philosophical system that

Maimonides confronted (e.g. **Aristotelianism**) was outdated. Yet, Krochmal envisages his own project to be identical to that of Maimonides: to provide a mechanism whereby traditional Jews can remain steadfast to their religious commitment in the light of modern intellectual challenges. In order to do this he has to reinterpret and re-signify the religious and intellectual significance of traditional religious forms. For instance, whereas Kant is critical of the heteronomous quality of Jewish law, Krochmal responds by arguing that this law, when properly understood, is not enslaving or coercive, but leads the individual to spiritual fulfilment. Krochmal is also interested in **history**, which, for him, enables the **Jewish people** to constantly renew itself.

See **autonomy**; **Enlightenment**; **Geiger, Abraham**; **Hegel, Georg Wilhelm Friedrich**; **history**; **Ibn Ezra, Abraham**; **Jewish people**; **Kant, Immanuel**; **Maimonides, Moses**; **Spinoza, Baruch**; **Wissenschaft des Judentums**

Further reading: Harris 1991

Leibowitz, Yeshayahu (1903–94) focused, unlike many of his twentieth-century contemporaries, on Judaism as an authentic possibility for an autonomous political community. He wrote from Israel, not the diaspora, and his thought needs to be contextualised within the various religio-political debates of that country. Because of his concern for individual authenticity, Leibowitz is an Existentialist, one who emphasised the centrality of the **halakhah** in Jewish life. Similar to **Maimonides** before him, Leibowitz argues for a type of **negative theology**, that is, it is impossible to speak of or describe God; one can only act before God's presence. He, thus, refuses to endow events (e.g. **the Shoah**, the foundation of the **state of Israel**) with value; for him, such value is not intrinsic to history or events, but can only be found in service to God, as defined by the parameters of the halakhah. He is, thus, critical of contemporary Jewish thinkers who try to reform Jewish law, which he perceives to be a matter of accommodation to modern non-Jewish society.

See **commandments; Existentialism; God, knowledge of; halakhah; history; Kaplan, Mordechai; Kook, Rav; negative theology; Talmud; Torah; Zionism**

Levinas, Emmanuel (1906–95) examined **ethics** from the perspective of the phenomenology of Husserl and **Heidegger**. He was, however, extremely critical and mistrustful of Heidegger, especially what he considered to be the lack of concern with **ethics** in his ontology. In his *Totality and Infinity* (*Totalité et infini*), Levinas builds on the thought of **Martin Buber** by arguing that we become whole only through encounters with others. Unlike Buber, however, Levinas argues that the 'I' in the I–Thou relationship is not reciprocal (as it is for Buber), but asymmetrical. The ideal I–Thou (in French, Je–Vous) relationship does not exist for itself, but solely for the thou.

In his *Otherwise than Being* (*Autrement qu'être*), he argues that the other puts demands on the self to such an extent that the self's very being is put into question in the encounter. I do not become whole simply by constituting myself as a self, but I do so only through the ethical relationship that I form with others. This leads to a situation in which I ultimately feel more responsibility for the other than I do for myself. Through the other, one encounters **transcendence**; it is for this reason that Levinas calls ethics 'first philosophy' for it is in the face of the other that one encounters God's **revelation**. Levinas finds this link between ethics, social justice and transcendence in the language of Judaism, which he expounds in works such as *Nine Talmudic Readings* (*Quatre lectures talmudiques*). Levinas has had an influence on both Jewish and non-Jewish thought, from theology to what is called continental philosophy.

See **autonomy; Buber, Martin; ethics; God, knowledge of; Post-Modernism; Talmud**

Further reading: Cohen 1994; Frank and Leaman 1997

logic: The science of logic has its origins in Aristotle, who used it to distinguish a good from a bad argument. A good argument is one that has an appropriate form (e.g. A belongs to all B; B belongs to all C; therefore, A belongs to all C). In the medieval period, logic is regarded as the science that functions as the gateway to all other sciences (e.g. **physics** and **metaphysics**). Even informed critics of philosophy, such as **Alghazali** and **Judah Halevi**, contend that logic is a valid science because they also have to acknowledge that there is a difference between a true argument and a false one. Logical arguments are often used in developing proofs for God's existence. The logical curriculum of the Middle Ages is essentially that part of the Aristotelian corpus known as the *Organon* (which included the books of Rhetoric and Poetics). This was often combined with the Arabic commentaries especially those of **Alfarabi** and **Averroes**. There is nothing particularly 'Jewish' about logic, and most Jews who engaged in philosophy studied logic with the help of these commentaries. One of **Maimonides**' earliest works was the *Treatise on Logic* (*Millot ha-Higgayon*), written in Arabic. In the nineteenth century, logic became increasingly symbolic and mathematical. So rather than envisage logic as a prolegomenon to philosophy, thinkers such as **Hermann Cohen** regard logic, the systematic study of pure thinking, as one of the primary branches of philosophy.

See **Alfarabi; Aristoteliansim; Averroes; Cohen, Hermann; God, arguments for the existence of; Halevi, Judah; Maimonides, Moses; rhetoric**
Further reading: Black 1990; Samuelson 1989

Maimonidean controversies: After the death of Maimonides, his ideas and rationalist programme spread very quickly owing to 'popularisers' such as **Shem Tov ibn Falaquera** who wrote in **Hebrew** and non-technically. This spread of Maimonidean teachings was also accompanied by a number of 'esotericists', such as Samuel **ibn Tibbon,** who radicalised Maimonides' thought by stressing its esoteric dimensions. The result was a backlash, expressed through a series of communal and personal conflicts that erupted during the thirteenth and fourteenth centuries. Critics argued that philosophy in general and Maimonideanism in particular spread confusion and weakened allegiance to Judaism. The main focus of these debates concerned the role and place of non-Jewish works and ideas in Judaism.

These Maimonidean controversies were not simply academic disagreements, but passionate and acrimonious debates about the proper orientation of Jewish culture. The controversies surrounding the teachings of Maimonides had begun just before his death when Maimonides was criticised for holding the unorthodox position that denied bodily resurrection in the **afterlife,** to which Maimonides responded with his *Epistle on Resurrection*, arguing that he affirmed bodily resurrection, but (1) the precise nature of it is unknown to humans and (2) the ultimate end of human life is the immortality of the perfected intellect, not the resurrection of the body.

The 'second phase' of these controversies occurred in Provence between 1232 and 1235, and focused on Maimonides' position on **creation** and **miracles**. This led to a number of counter-excommunications between pro-Maimonideans and anti-Maimonideans (who even denounced Maimonides' writings to the Catholic Church, thus involving the Church in internal Jewish affairs), and culminated in a ban on the study of philosophy.

The 'third phase' of the controversies occurred in Italy between 1288 and 1291 focusing primarily on the role of **allegory** and the biblical text. The 'final phase' occurred between 1305 and 1336 and revolved around the role of **astrology**, with anti-Maimonideans accusing philosophers of relying on the movement of the stars and thus being guilty of idolatry. This culminated in the ban on the study of philosophy for those under the age of twenty-five. An important alternative to rationalism in these controversies was the **kabbalah**, which was presented as an authentic Jewish tradition, upholding traditional doctrines and beliefs.

See **Abravanel, Isaac; afterlife; Aristotelianism; belief; commandments; conversion; creation; Crescas, Hasdai; divine will; eternity; gentiles; God, knowledge of; God, nature of; happiness; Ibn Falaquera, Shem Tov; Ibn Kaspi, Joseph; Ibn Tibbons; Jewish people; kabbalah; Maimonides, Moses; Messianic Era; miracles; omnipotence; omniscience; prophecy; reason; revelation; Torah**

Further reading: Frank and Leaman 1997; Guttmann 1964; Kellner 1986 and 1991; Kreisel 2001; Leaman 1997; Reines 1970; Silver 1965; Sirat 1985; Tirosh-Rothschild 1991; Tirosh-Samuelson 2003; H.A. Wolfson 1957

Maimonides, Moses (1138–1204) is the most important thinker in the history of Jewish philosophy. All critics of the rationalistic project (e.g. **Hasdai Crescas** and **Isaac Abravanel**) have to confront the writings of Maimonides. Furthermore, even modern philosophers, such as **Spinoza** or **Rosenzweig**, ultimately have to struggle with his legacy. He was born in Cordoba but his family was forced to flee when he was thirteen; they travelled around Southern Spain, settled in the Fez, where it is uncertain if the family had to 'convert' temporarily to Islam for pragmatic reasons. Eventually Maimonides settled in Egypt, where he became the leader of the Jewish community, in addition to being one of the most important court physicians in Cairo.

Maimonides wrote many works in disparate forms: *responsa* literature (legal rulings written in response to questions posed by Jewish communities), letters, commentaries, medical and logical treatises. His two most famous works, however, are the massive *Mishneh Torah*, which offers a systematisation and summary of the Oral **Torah**, and the philosophical *Guide of the Perplexed* (*Moreh ha-Nevukhim*). Whereas the former is written in Hebrew and is geared for all, the latter is written in Arabic (but translated into Hebrew by Samuel **ibn Tibbon**) and is written for a specific student (and those like him). For Maimonides, philosophy is not foreign to Judaism, but is the method that directs Jews to the level of proper worship. The first book of the *Mishneh Torah*, for example, opens by establishing God as the First Cause. With this, Maimonides makes philosophy integral to Judaism, and those Jews who do not have a proper understanding of the divine are guilty of idolatry.

The *Guide of the Perplexed* in many ways builds on this idea, but at a more advanced level. The *Guide* essentially presents the ideal reader with a key to unlock the philosophical mysteries of the Torah. A proper understanding of the Torah, for example, leads the ideal believer to realise that all of the **commandments** are given to the **Jewish people** for their intellectual perfection. The task of each Jew is to discover the meanings behind these commandments, ideally through a mastery of the various sciences. This, in so far as is humanly possibly, leads to the knowledge of God, which Maimonides equates with the love of God.

See **Abravanel, Isaac; Abulafia, Abraham; Alfarabi; allegoresis; Aristotelianism; commandments; creation; divine attributes; dogma; ethics; Genesis; God, arguments for the existence of; God, knowledge of; God, love of; God, nature of; happiness; Ibn Daud, Abraham; Ibn Tibbons; intellect; Jewish people; Maimonidean controversies; matter; Messianic Era; miracles; Moses; negative theology; political philosophy; prophecy; providence; rational mysticism; religious language; Scholasticism; Sinai; soul; Spinoza, Baruch; Strauss, Leo; Torah**

Further reading: Frank and Leaman 1997 and 2003; Green 1993; Guttmann 1964; Harris 1991; Hughes 2004b; Idel 1989; Kellner 1986 and 1991; Kraemer 1991; Kreisel 1999 and 2001; Leaman 1997; Preus 2001; Reines 1970; Rudavsky 2000; Seeskin 2000 and 2001; Silver 1965; Sirat 1985; Tirosh-Rothschild 1991; Tirosh-Samuelson 2003; Twersky 1980; H.A. Wolfson 1957

matter: According to medieval thinkers, following Aristotle, matter is one aspect of individual substances (e.g. Shmuel); the other aspect is **form**. Matter, then, is the capacity to receive properties, but it itself does not have any such properties. Matter, thus, functions as the common substratum of everything existing in the sublunar world, and, once form is added to it, it becomes a particular substance: so although all humans have the same form, they differ in terms of matter and the accidents (e.g. skin colour) inhering in it. Since form is permanent, matter is what is ultimately responsible for generation and corruption. For this reason, many were extremely critical of matter. **Maimonides,** for example, claims that it is matter that prevents us from intellectual apprehension of God. Others, especially those influenced by the Muslim **kalam,** argue that God constantly creates everything anew through matter, conceived of as atoms. Increasingly in the early modern period, matter is regarded as having essential properties.

See **Alghazali; Asharites; atomism; emanation; evil, problem of; form; kalam; Maimonides, Moses; Mutazilites; Neoplatonism; Platonism**

Mendelssohn, Moses (1729–86) was one of the earliest representatives of the Jewish **Enlightenment**. He essentially tried to balance the rationalist metaphysics of Leibniz and Wolff with the dictates of Judaism. In 1763 he won first prize over a paper submitted by **Immanuel Kant** in an essay competition sponsored by the Berlin Academy of Sciences. Despite this, Mendelssohn never fully integrated into Berlin society owing to its general intolerance of Judaism. Shortly after his victory in the essay competition, a Christian preacher by the name of Lavater sent Mendelssohn a book he had just translated along with a note that he hoped that the book would persuade him to convert to Christianity.

Mendelssohn spent most of the rest of his life responding to this challenge in various ways. His most forceful response is found in what is considered to be his most famous work, *Jerusalem, Or On Religious Power and Judaism* (*Jerusalem, oder über religiose Macht und Judenthum*), in which he makes his case for Judaism as a religion of reason, but one that is nonetheless distinct from other religions. In particular, he argues that Judaism is not a revealed religion that demands that Jews passively accept a set of dogmas, but a 'revealed legislation' that requires the performance of particular actions. He posits that at **Sinai** the Israelites already possessed the universal principles of Judaism as a natural religion (i.e. those truths that are comprehensible and demonstrable by reason not revelation), but that what they received there was the ceremonial law in order to help them remember constantly the dictates of natural religion and to discourage idolatry. This rational, moral and natural Judaism – Mendelssohn claims – belongs at the heart of the modern European state.

Mendelssohn also published German translations of a number of biblical books (including the **Torah,** or five books of Moses), in addition to a **commentary** on it, called *Bi'ur*. His goal in doing this was to get German Jews to give up Yiddish and replace it with both German and Hebrew.

See **anti-Semitism; autonomy; commentary; Enlightenment; God, arguments for the existence of; Krochmal, Nachman; monotheism; reason; Torah; Wissenschaft des Judentums**

Further reading: Altmann 1973; Frank and Leaman 1997; Guttmann 1964; Meyer 1967; Samuelson 1989; Seeskin 2001; Sorkin 1996

Messer Leon, David ben Judah (c. 1470–c. 1535) was born in Venice and, like most elite Jews of the Renaissance, was educated in **halakhah,** medieval philosophy and humanism. Most importantly, though, he was one of the first Jewish Aristotelian thinkers to study the **kabbalah.** He subsequently moved to Naples and, with the expulsion of the Jews from there in 1495, he made his way East, to the Ottoman Empire. There he became one of the most important scholars in Ottoman Jewry. He wrote, among other things, *The Shield of David* (*Magen David*) and *Glory to David* (*Tehilah le-David*). David ben Judah is an important transitional figure because in his writings we witness the shift from **Aristotelianism** to kabbalah. His innovation is that philosophy and kabbalah are compatible with one another because the kabbalah should be interpreted philosophically. As a result, he develops a theoretical model that enables this to happen. For example, he interprets the divine sefirot in light of the discussion of the **divine attributes**. His subsequent philosophisation of the kabbalah was instrumental in the dissemination of the kabbalah in Italy and the Ottoman Empire.

See **Abravanel, Judah; Alemanno, Yohanan; Aristotelianism; Ficino, Marsilio; God, nature of; kabbalah; Messer Leon, Judah; Pico della Mirandola, Giovanni; rational mysticism**

Further reading: Tirosh-Rothschild 1991

Messer Leon, Judah (c. 1425–c. 95) was an Aristotelian philosopher and one of the most important Jewish thinkers of the fifteenth century. The father of **David ben Judah Messer Leon**, he received a doctoral degree in philosophy and medicine from the German Emperor, Frederick III, which was a very rare honour granted to a Jew. This enabled him to award doctoral degrees to other students, which he did, one of the most famous being **Yohanan Alemanno**. He wrote a commentary to Porphyry's *Isagoge*, a biblical commentary, a commentary to the *Guide of the Perplexed*, and an important work of Jewish rhetoric, *The Book of the Honeycomb's Flow* (*Sefer Nopheth Tsufim*), modelled on the genre of the art of rhetoric common in the Italian Renaissance. Judah Messer Leon also issued an edict banning **Gersonides**' commentary to the Torah, which he regarded as too philosophical and, thus, subversive. He was also critical of the **kabbalah** for being too subversive and logically unclear. This was met with great opposition by other rabbis, who argued that he was trying to establish his own authority over Italian Jewry.

See **Abravanel, Judah; Alemanno, Yohanan; Aristotelianism; Ficino, Marsilio; Gersonides; kabbalah; Messer Leon, David ben Judah; Maimonidean controversies**

Further reading: Tirosh-Rothschild 1991

Messianic Era: Although traditional Judaism does not speak with one voice about the Messianic Era, most agree that it will be a time unlike the present, and that it will involve the rebuilding of the Temple, the restoration of the Davidic monarchy, the resurrection of the dead, and that it will culminate in a day of judgement.

Most philosophers, especially those under the influence of **Aristotelianism**, tend to naturalise the concept of the Messianic Era. **Maimonides**, for example, argues that the Messianic period will be continuous with world **history**, with the significant exception that the Jews will have political independence in their own land. In like manner, **Gersonides** claims that the Messianic Era will also be one of political autonomy, an era in which the **providence** that the **Jewish people** have inherited from Abraham will enable them to live in their own land and receive providence based on their own merits. Other philosophers, in particular those influenced by **astrology** such as **Abraham bar Hiyya**, try to predict the date of the arrival of the Messiah.

Among modern Jewish philosophers, **Franz Rosenzweig** is the one most interested in the nature of the Messianic Era. For him, the goal towards which the universe moves is one of unity, in which God, humanity and the world will become one. This will establish a living world in which God becomes redeemed and humans strive to be like God.

See **afterlife; Aristotelianism; astrology; Bar Hiyya, Abraham; Gersonides; happiness; history; Jewish people; Maimonidean controversies; Maimonides, Moses; political philosophy; Rosenzweig, Franz**

Further reading: Eisen 1995; Feldman 2003; Kellner 1986 and 1991; Kreisel 1999 and 2001; Myers 2003; Samuelson 1989

metaphor: A figure of speech in which one word is used in place of another to denote a likeness between them. For example, the phrase 'love is a rose' intimates that love is something beautiful, precious, yet also fleeting. Implicit in this definition is that metaphors are representative of non-literal or figurative speech. Many philosophers, in both the medieval and modern periods, contend that the only way in which we can speak about God is through metaphors, which approximate but do not limit God. In their allegorical readings of the Bible, for example, words such as God's 'hand' can be seen as metaphors for God's providence.

See **allegoresis; allegory; God, knowledge of; negative theology**

metaphysics: In broad terms, the investigation of the nature of reality, especially the structure of the universe. The main metaphysical question of the medieval Neoplatonists was: how and why does plurality exist if everything emanates from the unity of the One? Some, such as **Isaac Israeli**, argue that God created first **form** and first **matter** ex nihilo. Later Neoplatonists build on and modify this through their respective theories of **emanation**, but the problem still remains: if the One is incorporeal, from where does corporeality come? Jewish Aristotelians pick up where the Neoplatonists leave off, arguing for a series of **emanations** that come from the One, with difference in this world predicated on the instability of matter, in which various accidents occur. This, however, is met with sharp criticism by critics of **Aristotelianism** such as **Hasdai Crescas**, who try to dismantle Aristotle's metaphysics by deconstructing the natural principles upon which it is founded.

Immanuel Kant is usually regarded as the destroyer of metaphysics, at least as traditionally understood. Most modern Jewish philosophers are, in the aftermath of Kant, more interested in **ethics** than metaphysics, working on the assumption that the existence of God is a necessary postulate for making sense of our duties under moral law.

See **Active Intellect; Aristotelianism; Avicenna; cosmology; creation; emanation; essence and existence; ethics; form; Halevi, Judah; Israeli, Isaac; kabbalah; Kant, Immanuel; negative theology; Neoplatonism; physics; Platonism; Plotinus; soul**

Further reading: Fakhry 1983; Frank and Leaman 1997 and 2003; Goodman 1992; Harvey 1998; Hayoun 1986; Hughes 2004a; Kraemer 1991; Rauschenbach 2002; Rudavsky 2000; Winston 1985; E. R. Wolfson 1994; H. A. Wolfson 1957 and 1975

midrash (pl. midrashim): Traditional rabbinic interpretations of the Bible; they can be of either a legal (midrash halakhah) or non-legal (midrash aggadah) variety. The latter are homilies on biblical verses, and they form part of traditional Jewish literature that includes ethical maxims, popular sayings, folklore, stories of miracles, etc. The main philosophical problem with midrashim, especially of the aggadic variety, is that they describe God in grossly anthropomorphic and anthropopathic terms, which many philosophers considered to be beyond the bounds of good sense. Both **Karaites** and Muslims, for example, were extremely critical of this literature as, among other things, pointing to Judaism's lack of intellectual development. The main philosophical response to this literature was that it could not be understood literally. **Maimonides**, for example, contends that many aggadic midrashim contain philosophical truths that, like the Bible itself, have to be decoded. This idea is shared by **Emil Fackenheim**, who argues that midrash represents a non-discursive language that allowed Jews to describe their encounter with God and particular momentous events in the best way that they could.

See **allegoresis; allegory; Fackenheim, Emil; hermeneutics; parables; Plaskow, Judith; Talmud; Torah**

miracles: If God is responsible for the natural order, why would he violate this order? If God, as an **intellect** engaged in constant self-intellection, is unconcerned with the ebb and flow of particular individuals, why or how would he intervene in human **history**? At the same time, however, the biblical record is full of the miraculous, for example, the parting of the Sea of Reeds, the stopping of the sun. The concept of miracles is intimately connected to the questions of **creation** and **prophecy**. If the world is eternal, this would seem to curtail God's ability to act freely in the world. Similarly, if miracles occur when prophets are around, the relationship between the prophet and the miraculous has to be established.

To confront these problems, Jewish philosophers have offered many, often competing, responses. One is that the miraculous exists and that God is the direct cause of such miracles (e.g. **Judah Halevi, Nahmanides, Isaac Abravanel**). Another response is that it is not God but the **Active Intellect** that is responsible for miracles when the prophet, qua individual with superior intellect, is able to activate a series of laws that exist within the Active Intellect (e.g. **Gersonides**). Yet another response is that God placed miracles within the natural order at the beginning of time, so that when they occurred later it would appear as if they occurred based on an immediate need (this is the opinion of **Maimonides**, at least in his *Commentary to the Mishnah*).

See **Abravanel, Isaac**; **Active Intellect**; **Asharites**; cosmology; creation; divine will; emanation; **Gersonides**; God, nature of; **Halevi, Judah**; history; intellect; **Maimonidean controversies**; **Maimonides, Moses**; **Messianic Era**; **Nahmanides**; nature; prophecy; revelation; **Spinoza, Baruch**

Further reading: Eisen 1995; Feldman 2003; Frank and Leaman 1997 and 2003; Harvey 1998; Hayoun 1986; Kellner 1986; Kreisel 2001; Lawee 2001; Reines 1970; Silver 1965

Mishnah see **Talmud**; **Torah**

monotheism: The idea of a single God who is transcendent to the world is as central to Jewish philosophy as it is to Judaism. Jewish philosophers, however, conceive of monotheism in terms that are often distinct from those used in traditional or rabbinic Judaism. God, for example, can in no way be regarded as a 'super-man' (e.g. a Zeus-like figure), someone who possesses feelings or emotions in the same way that humans do.

The medieval Neoplatonists and Aristotelians agree that it is necessary to conceive of God as First Cause, about which we can essentially know nothing, a cause that by thinking Itself produces or generates the universe. Since this God does not willfully intervene in the affairs of this world, any positive knowledge of God is impossible. For this reason, many were emphatic that all that we can know about God is what he is not. To say that God possesses 'life', for example, is to negate in him the trait of death – all the while realising that saying 'God lives' is radically different from saying that 'Saul lives'.

Modern Jewish philosophers, influenced by the thought of **Immanuel Kant**, stress the notion of 'ethical monotheism', by which they usually mean that the ideal conception of monotheism creates and sustains a moral imperative that governs human action. **Hermann Cohen**, for example, argues that ethical monotheism, which functions as the ideal conception of God, is unique to Judaism. For **Rosenzweig**, God is also an infinite essence, completely different from all that is not-God; the only way for humans to have a relationship with God is through the world, not in the sense of **Spinoza's pantheism**, but in the sense that humans act upon the world to redeem it through community, language and ritual practice.

See **Aristotelianism; Buber, Martin; Cohen, Hermann; cosmology; divine attributes; divine will; emanation; God, nature of; intellect; Kant, Immanuel; Neoplatonism; omnipotence; omniscience; pantheism; Spinoza, Baruch; transcendence**

Further reading: Seeskin 2000

Moses is the prophet responsible for the reception of the **Torah** at Sinai. Since most Jewish philosophers regard the Torah as the blueprint for **happiness**, Moses' prophecy is regarded as both quantitatively and qualitatively different from that of the other prophets. If prophets are regarded as philosophers in the sense that they possess intellectual (and imaginative) perfection, then Moses becomes the philosopher *par excellence*. On one level this is a difficult argument to make because obviously Moses was not a scientist.

Many of the medieval philosophers create taxonomies of prophets, describing the various levels that each prophet attained to. **Isaac Israeli**, for example, argues that Moses reached the highest level of prophecy, that of speech, which is tantamount to union with the divine. **Maimonides** claims that the **imagination** played no part in Moses' reception of the Torah, unlike the case with the other prophets. Moses did, however, use his imagination in transmitting the teachings to the Israelites. Although Spinoza calls Moses' intellectual perfection and authorship of the Torah into question, most subsequent Jewish philosophers tend to be more interested in the product of Moses' prophecy, the Torah, than his actual person.

See **belief; Cohen, Hermann; happiness; imagination; intellect; Israeli, Isaac; Maimonides, Moses; political philosophy; prophecy; Sinai; Spinoza, Baruch; Torah**

Further reading: Eisen 1995; Kreisel 1999 and 2001; Tirosh-Samuelson 2003

Mutazilites: The Mutazilites were the first school of **kalam** (systematic theology) in Islam. They stressed God's unity and justice, and that reason could guide humans to salvation. They also argued that divine speech (e.g. the Koran) was a created accident and could not be regarded as eternal, which would limit God's own eternality. In the ninth century, they set up an inquisition in which every judge had to swear that they believed the Koran was created; if they did not, they were dismissed and thrown into jail.

The Mutazilites exerted significant influence on early Jewish rational theologians, most notably **Saadia Gaon.** Saadia, however, was not particularly interested in the status of God's speech, and he regarded revelation as a temporal creation that had to be reconciled with God's eternal nature. In his discussion of the kalam in *Guide* 1: 71, **Maimonides** argues that the Mutazilites and others are not true philosophers, but people who used rational argumentation in the service of defending their religious traditions. He accuses them of manipulating their premises to fit their pre-established conclusions. Although the Mutazilites fell out of favour in Islam, many of their theological premises were adopted by the **Karaites**.

See **Asharites; atomism; determinism; free will; God, nature of; kalam; Karaites; Saadia Gaon**

Further reading: Fakhry 1983; Frank and Leaman 1997 and 2003; Leaman and Nasr 1996; Pines 1997; Sirat 1985

mysticism see **Abulafia, Abraham; Alemanno, Yohanan; kabbalah; Nahmanides; rational mysticism**

Nahmanides (1194–1270) was born in a Christian environment, learned in both the Judeo-Arabic philosophical tradition and traditional rabbinic thought. He was also largely responsible for the emergence and popularity of **kabbalah** at the end of the thirteenth century. As the central rabbi in Catalonia, he played a moderating role in the **Maimonidean controversy** of 1232; he was also involved in an official disputation put on by the Catholic Church in Barcelona, where he had to defend Judaism publicly against a Jewish apostate, Pablo Christiani.

Nahmanides is a very complicated thinker. On the one hand he is a conservative thinker critical of rationalism; yet, on the other hand, he tried to prevent the banning of **Maimonides'** *Guide* outright and frequently used rational argumentation in his biblical commentaries. For example, he claims, like Maimonides, that Talmudic aggadot (rabbinic tales) and **midrashim** should be interpreted non-literally. But, whereas Maimonides had argued that the deepest level of the **Torah** is equivalent to **physics** and **metaphysics**, Nahmanides contends that at the heart of the Torah there resides many of the mystical and theosophical principles associated with the kabbalah.

Nahmanides is particularly critical of the philosophical discussion of **miracles**. For him, miracles are either 'revealed' or 'hidden': the former, such as the splitting of the Sea of Reeds cannot be explained by nature, but only by divine intervention; the latter are manifest in terms of rewards and punishments, and although they appear to violate no natural laws they nevertheless show God's direct involvement in the affairs of this world, especially those of the **Jewish people**. For Nahmanides, the discussion of miracles presupposes the creation of the universe.

His biblical commentaries – involving literal, moral and mystical interpretations – were among the first to apply kabbalistic readings in a setting that was meant for all to read. Like Maimonides, he is interested in the reasons behind the **commandments**; but, unlike him, these reasons are mystical and **theurgical**, not political or commemorative.

See **commandments; commentary; creation; God, nature of; Jewish people; kabbalah; Maimonidean controversies; Maimonides, Moses; midrash; miracles; theurgy**

Further reading: Frank and Leaman 1997; Tirosh-Samuelson 2003

Narboni, Moses (d. 1362) primarily wrote commentaries to other treatises such as *The Guide of the Perplexed*, and the works of **Averroes**, **Alghazali** and **Ibn Tufayl**. He also composed three original treatises: the *Epistle on the Shiur Qoma* (*Iggeret Shiur Qoma*), *Treatise on Free Will* (*Ma'amar ha-Behira*) and *The Chapters of Moshe* (*Pirkei Moshe*).

The basis of Narboni's system is that the world is not created in time but is eternally produced by God as First Cause. For Narboni, this is not heretical; rather, it makes

God the cause of the world in more complex ways than if he had created it in time since God must continually give the world existence. God not only sustains the world, but also gives it all of its forms, including the form of matter. Following Averroes, Narboni argues that happiness resides in conjunction with the Active Intellect; when an individual has achieved this level of conjunction, he is able to manipulate material objects, thereby making miracles possible.

Narboni is also interested in fitting terminology associated with the kabbalah into philosophical categories. In this, it seems that he was inspired by various cryptic comments scattered throughout the writings of Abraham ibn Ezra. In his commentary of Ibn Tufayl's *Hayy ibn Yaqzan*, for example, Narboni equates the sefirot of the kabbalah with the ten separate intellects of medieval Aristotelianism.

See Abner of Burgos; Active Intellect; Alghazali; Averroes; commentary; creation, eternal; Crescas, Hasdai; form; God, knowledge of; God, nature of; happiness; Ibn Ezra, Abraham; Ibn Kaspi, Joseph; Ibn Tufayl; intellect; Maimonidean controversies; Maimonides, Moses; matter; rational mysticism

Further reading: Frank and Leaman 1997 and 2003; Guttmann 1964; Hayoun 1986; Sirat 1985

nationalism see Zionism

nature: Most medieval philosophers regard the world of nature as the outcome of emanation. This world is then governed by means of laws that are responsible for various natural causes. For Maimonides, the regularity of these natural laws proclaims the majesty of God more clearly than their violation (i.e. in the case of miracles). At the same time, however, there exists a certain mistrust about the world of nature because it is, after all, composed of matter, whose instability is ultimately responsible for the generation and corruption of all material things. Those thinkers influenced by **astrology** (e.g. **Abraham ibn Ezra**) argue that the world of nature came under the influence of the heavenly spheres and planetary motions. By the fifteenth century, when philosophy and **kabbalah** increasingly began to fuse together, thinkers such as **Judah Abravanel** put more of an emphasis on God's immanence in the world of nature. This stream of thought reaches its pinnacle when **Spinoza** equates God with nature (*Deus, sive Natura*), making God not the creator of the heavens and the earth, but an extended substance immanent throughout the world of nature. **Martin Buber**, although not going as far as this, claims that it is in the world of nature that the individual begins to enter the dialogue with God as the 'Eternal Thou'.

See **Abravanel, Judah; aesthetics; Aristotelianism; astrology; Buber, Martin; cosmology; creation; emanation; eternity; God, knowledge of; God, nature of; kabbalah; Maimonides, Moses; Neoplatonism; physics; Platonism; Spinoza, Baruch**

negative theology: Most medieval philosophers posit a large gap between human and divine knowledge, with the only commonality between them being the noun 'knowledge'. The term negative theology is most often associated with **Maimonides**, who argues that God is utterly transcendent and irreducible to anything in the material world. As such, any language used to describe God must be employed with extreme caution. Any term predicated of God's essence (e.g. one, eternal, living) must be regarded as nothing more than the denial of imperfection. To say that 'God is living', for example, does not mean that God lives in the same way that you or I do, but that God is 'not dead'.

In like manner, all non-essential attributes (e.g. anger, merciful, just) are regarded as **divine attributes** of action. For example, to say that 'God is merciful' means that God acts in such a manner that is analogous to actions that express the human notion of mercy. Maimonides' caution with regard to such discourse is to protect God's absolute simplicity and incorporeality, so that humans do not regard him as a larger version of themselves (i.e. in much the way that the Greeks understood their gods). Not everyone agreed with Maimonides, however. Many mystics influenced by the **kabbalah,** for instance, claim to know God's essence and they argued that every Jew was involved in an ongoing cosmic drama. Philosophically, **Gersonides** contends that God's knowledge is not completely different from human knowledge, and that God does have knowledge of particulars. The modern version of negative theology is best expressed in the thought of **Franz Rosenzweig,** who argues that God is not limited by anything and that God is ultimately defined by a negation, that is, everything that is not-God.

See **allegory; Gersonides; God, knowledge of; God, nature of; kabbalah; Maimonides, Moses; metaphor; religious language; Rosenzweig, Franz**

Further reading: Kraemer 1991; Seeskin 2000

Neoplatonism is a very difficult term to grasp, because, although it is customarily employed to refer to the late antique and medieval periods, it is actually a modern term. The result is that no thinker in the aforementioned periods would have considered himself to be a 'Neoplatonist'; rather, they would most likely have considered themselves to be engaged in a project of expounding Plato's thought by means of various doctrines attributed to Aristotle and other ancient authors. The 'founder' of Neoplatonism is usually regarded as **Plotinus**, whose work was falsely attributed to Aristotle in the medieval period. Indeed, it is probably better to speak of 'Neoplatonic schools' as opposed to the Neoplatonic school. Some Neoplatonists considered **theurgy** to be a valid form of philosophy, whereas others regarded it as a degenerate practice. Neoplatonism was not just about philosophy, but was also a religious movement that promised its adherents a strict regimen of life, one that culminated in salvation.

Two ideas central to Neoplatonism in all of its various manifestations are the doctrine of **emanation** and the 'myth of the **soul**'. According to this myth, the soul is intimately and ontically related to the Universal Soul, from which it departs to reside in a human body. Trapped in this body, the soul can either aspire to reascend to its celestial home or become mired in the filth of matter. The way for the soul to reascend is by means of the study of philosophy. Typical Jewish Neoplatonists include **Isaac Israeli, Shlomo ibn Gabirol**, and **Abraham ibn Ezra**. Eventually in the late twelfth century, Neoplatonism gradually gave way to **Aristotelianism**, although the fact that Plotinus' work circulated under the name of Aristotle still meant that most Aristotelians, including **Maimonides**, still incorporated Neoplatonic elements into their thought.

See **Active Intellect; Alfarabi; Aristotelianism; Avicenna; creation; emanation; evil, problem of; God, knowledge of; God, nature of; Ibn Daud, Abraham; Ibn Gabirol, Shlomo; Ibn Ezra, Abraham; Israeli, Isaac; Platonism; Plotinus; rational mysticism; soul; theurgy**

Further reading: Fakhry 1983; Frank and Leaman 1997 and 2003; Guttmann 1964; Hughes 2004a; Kraemer 1991; Kreisel 2001; Lobel 2000; Sirat 1985; Tanenbaum 2002; E. R. Wolfson 1994

Neopythagoreanism is a modern term employed by scholars to denote the revival of the thought of Pythagoras in the first century BCE. In many ways it is indistinguishable from Middle Platonism, except for the fact that it regards Pythagoras as a quasi-prophet and the source of all true wisdom. By the third century, teachings of the Neopythagoreans had essentially been absorbed into those of **Neoplatonism**. Neopythagoreanism is primarily associated with a **metaphysics** of mathematics, in which the number one, as a transcendent principle, is responsible for bringing the world and matter into existence. Neopythagoreanism is also characterised by it emphasis on the immortality of the **soul**, and the transmigration of souls.

Neopythagorean ideas were common in the thought of the **Ikhwan al-Safa'**, who stress that God is the first principle of all things in the same way that the number one is the first principle of all numbers. They also equate mathematics with a proper understanding of the soul: he who properly understands numbers is able to comprehend the ways in which accidents adhere to substances. The thought of the Ikhwan influenced many of the Jewish Neoplatonists, especially that of **Abraham ibn Ezra**, whose *Yesod Mora* discusses God's name and his unity using mathematical principles.

See **cosmology; God, knowledge of; God, nature of; Ibn Ezra, Abraham; Ikhwan al-Safa'; Platonism; Plotinus**

Further reading: Fakhry 1983; Leaman and Nasr 1996

Noahide laws: Refer to those laws given to Noah before the revelation to **Moses** at Sinai. Since Noah's sons included the descendents of **gentiles**, the Noahide laws are binding on all of humanity. In terms of the **Jewish people**, the Noahide laws were replaced by the commandments revealed at Sinai, but with some minor exceptions are subsumed into the commandments. The laws themselves consist of six prohibitions (against idolatry, murder, theft, blasphemy, eating the flesh of living animals, and sexual immorality) and one positive command to establish courts of justice to administer the law.

See **commandments; gentiles; Jewish people; Moses; Sinai; Torah**

occasionalism: The denial of natural causality (e.g. A causes B). It is a doctrine that is frequently appealed to in order to protect God's absolute supremacy and active and ongoing involvement in the world. Occasionalism is often coupled with **atomism**, the theory that God constantly renews the universe through the formation, dissolution and reformulation of atoms. Occasionalism proved to be a popular doctrine among the **Asharites**, but was given its most sustained and important discussion in the work of **Alghazali**. According to him, even though we think we see A cause B, this is only a perception and that the real cause of both is God such that B is produced concomitantly with A. Under different circumstances, therefore, A need not cause B. Even though we assume the sun will rise tomorrow because it always rises on a new day, in the occasionalist's universe there is no guarantee that the sun will rise tomorrow if God should will it otherwise. The benefit of this argument is that God can do anything at any time, making creation, miracles and prophecy dependent directly on God and not the rational laws of nature. Occasionalism did not make major inroads into Jewish thought. Even though some **Karaites** used theories of atomism, they tended to argue for natural causation.

See **Alghazali; Asharites; atomism; cosmology; God, nature of; kalam; Karaites; Mutazilites**

Further reading: Fakhry 1983; Leaman and Nasr 1996; Pines 1997

omnipotence: The idea that God, as the greatest Being possible, is all powerful. This causes a problem for philosophers: if God is all powerful, can he violate the laws of nature and do that which is logically impossible? Early Muslim theologians argued that God could ostensibly command anything (including murder) and, because it was God's command, it would have to be right. Jewish philosophers, like their Muslim counterparts, claim that this is ludicrous and, despite the fact that they recognise God as the most perfect Being, they nonetheless have to redefine the term omnipotence.

Most medieval philosophers posit that God is essentially an Intellect constantly thinking Itself. Since God is an Intellect and intellects, by nature, only know forms or universals, this would seem to imply that God could not know the particulars of the material world and, therefore, could not act in this world. It was up to the **Active Intellect** to 'watch over' and act in this world. Informed critics of philosophy, such as **Judah Halevi,** counter that the emanative **cosmology** of the philosophers limits God. Perhaps responding to this charge, **Maimonides** argues that God is omnipotent, but that the human intellect has no way of grasping what this term means with respect to God.

Increasingly in the modern period Jewish philosophers are less concerned with God's omnipotence than they are with his moral perfection as a model for human behaviour. A somewhat different account, however, is offered by **Mordechai Kaplan,** whose concept of Judaism as a civilisation is predicated on the notion that Jews historically have thought that God exists, although Kaplan himself is not concerned with how God exists or even if he actually does. Moreover, the **Shoah** leads a number of Jewish thinkers to question the traditional idea that God can act in history whenever he pleases.

See **Active Intellect; Aristotelianism; Cohen, Hermann; creation; divine will; emanation; God, nature of; Halevi, Judah; intellect; kalam; Kant, Immanuel; Kaplan, Mordechai; Maimonides, Moses; omniscience; religion; Shoah, the; Torah**

Further reading: Cohen 1994; Friedman 2002; Guttmann 1964; Kraemer 1991; Leaman 1997; Rauschenbach 2002; Reines 1970; Samuelson 2002; Seeskin 2000; H. A. Wolfson 1975

omniscience: The idea that God, as the greatest Being possible, is all knowing. This causes a problem for philosophers because if God knows everything, how can humans act freely? Since most medieval philosophers define God as an Intellect and intellects, by nature, only know forms or universals, then how can God know individuals. This position, then, would seem to curtail God's knowledge. This is perhaps put most forcefully in medieval Jewish philosophy by **Gersonides**, who posits that God knows the general laws governing human behaviour, but not whether a particular person will make a specific choice when faced with a particular decision. **Hasdai Crescas,** who upholds the notion that God does know everything, labels Gersonides' position heretical. Increasingly in the modern period Jewish philosophers are less concerned with God's omniscience than they are with his moral perfection as a model for human behaviour.

See **Active Intellect; Aristotelianism; Cohen, Hermann; compatibilism and incompatibilism; creation; divine will; emanation; God, nature of; Halevi, Judah;**

intellect; kalam; Kant, Immanuel; Kaplan, Mordechai; Maimonides, Moses; religion; Shoah, the; Torah

Further reading: Cohen 1994; Friedman 2002; Guttmann 1964; Kraemer 1991; Leaman 1997; Rauschenbach 2002; Reines 1970; Samuelson 2002; Seeskin 2000; H. A. Wolfson 1975

pantheism: The notion that God and the universe are one; as such, pantheists stress the concept of God's immanence in the world of nature at the expense of his transcendence. Most medieval Jewish philosophy is not pantheistic because it stresses the complete otherness and transcendence of God. Jewish mysticism, or **kabbalah**, in contrast, regards the cosmos as part of God, especially in the unfolding of unity into multiplicity. Although this is not pantheism per se, it does posit an intimate relationship between God and the world.

The most famous spokesperson for pantheism, however, is **Baruch Spinoza,** who equates God with **nature** (especially as formulated in his famous slogan *Deus, sive Natura* , 'God or Nature'). According to him, God or Nature is a substance in which all things partake; God, thus, becomes a cause immanent in all things. This concept of God, however, is not that of traditional Judaism: God ceases to be a creator, an object of worship or an actor in history. This formulation all but destroys the classical notion of God in both traditional Judaism and medieval Jewish philosophy.

Among modern Jewish philosophers, **Buber** contends that the only way to apprehend God is through the concrete relationships with physical others and the world of nature. Although such a view is not pantheism per se,

Buber does reconfigure the traditional account of God in such a way that God is not completely separate from this world. **Rosenzweig,** rebelling against the transcendental notion of God associated with **Idealism,** nevertheless still makes God completely separate from the world, with humans functioning as the bridge between them.

See **Aristotelianism; cosmology; dogma; emanation; God, nature of; kabbalah; monotheism; nature; Platonism; Plotinus; Rosenzweig, Franz; Spinoza, Baruch**

parables: Parables play an important role in pre-modern Jewish philosophy. Most Jewish philosophers from **Philo** to **Judah Abravanel** hold that the **Torah** is a perfect book that contains all of the secrets of philosophy. However, **Moses** had to convey these abstract truths in such a way that all of the **Jewish people** could grasp at least a modicum of such truths. Since the prophet is defined by the perfection of both his intellect and imagination, he can easily translate intelligibles into an attractive and easily accessible language. Because of this, most medieval philosophers argue that the Torah is an intricate set of parables that has to be decoded properly. A good example of this is the Song of Songs, whose outer form functions as an erotic love poem between two lovers. The rabbis had argued that this biblical book was an extended parable for the intimate relationship between God and Israel. Many of the philosophers, however, go even further and claim that it is actually a parable of the relationship between the individual **soul** and God. Parables are not the sole repository of the Torah; many philosophers themselves composed parables in order to convey philosophical truths only to those who had a requisite understanding of the various sciences. The best example of this is **Maimonides'** *Guide of the Perplexed*, the introduction to which describes his strategy for employing parables.

See **allegoresis; allegory; apologetics; hermeneutics; metaphor; midrash; Neoplatonism; Plotinus; religious language; rhetoric**

Philo of Alexandria (c. 15 BCE–c. 50 CE) was one of the earliest Jewish philosophers and the foremost representative of Judeo-Hellenistic thought. Although he is heavily indebted to the thought of Plato, his writings show an unwavering commitment to the Jewish tradition and the superiority of **Moses' prophecy**. The majority of his work is written in the form of **commentary**, in which he reads the biblical narrative allegorically. Philo's starting point is that only a life lived in accordance with reason leads to true **happiness**. The blueprint for this life is, not surprisingly, to be located in the Bible, but only when it is read properly.

Philo's overarching methodology is to read into the Bible philosophical concepts derived from the Greeks. For example, he redefines the God of the Bible as a self-sufficient and pure Being that exists beyond everything. Philo bridges the ontological gap between God and the universe through the concept of the Logos, a 'rational thought of mind expressed in utterance or speech'. In other words, the Logos is the speech or thought of God that exists throughout the rational order of the universe and is accessible to the human **intellect**. Although Philo puts great stock in human reason, he argues that the unaided human intellect cannot discover all of the laws of nature on its own. For this, it is dependant upon a divine law revealed by God to humans. Philo understands this law in terms of Platonic teachings: what Moses received on **Sinai** was knowledge of the incorporeal forms that he subsequently recorded allegorically. Thus, it becomes the task of the philosopher to uncover the true meanings behind these allegories.

Although Philo was largely unknown to subsequent Jews, and his thought exerted considerable impact on Christian philosophical teachings, his frames of reference are essentially those of all later medieval Jewish philosophers.

See **allegoresis; allegory; Aristobolus; commentary; God, knowledge of; God, nature of; happiness; metaphor; Moses; parables; Platonism; prophecy; religious language**

Further reading: Frank and Leaman 1997; Winston 1985; H. A. Wolfson 1975

physics: For the majority of medieval Jewish philosophers, physics refers to the world existing below the sphere of the moon (as opposed to **metaphysics**, which dealt with the universe above the sphere of the moon). Despite this, there exists an intimate connection between the two sciences because **matter** and **form** occupy all levels of reality, with the exception of God. Combining Aristotelian and Neoplatonic teachings, medieval Jewish philosophers tend to conceive of this world as composed of various mixtures of the four elements (i.e. earth, air, fire and water). Since **matter** is unstable it can take on various forms, a hierarchy of being emerges because matter can assume different degrees of corporeality.

Medieval philosophers posit a hierarchical universe in which everything occupied its natural place based on the telos of its species, with everything ranked on a 'great chain of being' from God to prime matter. According to **Maimonides**, physics is the science responsible for teaching us God's actions within the universe. **Gersonides,** for the most part, shares this view, but he claims, using Aristotle's *Physics*, that the world has to be created and that this **creation** could not be *ex nihilo*. In his debate with the philosophers, **Hasdai Crescas** tries to refute the Aristotelian physics upon which much of the medieval Jewish philosophical enterprise rested. For example, Crescas claims not only for the possibility but also for the existence of actual infinity.

See **Aristotelianism; atomism; cosmology; creation; Crescas, Hasdai; emanation; evil, problem of; form; Gersonides; God, knowledge of; God, nature of; Maimonides, Moses; matter; metaphysics; nature; Platonism**
Further reading: Harvey 1998; H. A. Wolfson 1957

Pico della Mirandola, Giovanni (1463–94) was one of the towering intellectual figures of the Italian Renaissance. Like most other Renaissance thinkers, Pico was more interested in the thought of Plato than Aristotle. He was deeply intrigued by the **kabbalah** and hired a number of Jewish thinkers (among them, **Yohanan Alemanno**) to teach him about its secrets. Pico's goal was to create a universal philosophical system in which all religious truth could be seen as pointing towards its natural telos in Christianity. On one level, Pico was very interested in Judaism and Jewish teaching, but, on the other, he ultimately used his philosophical system to try and convert Jews to his vision of Christianity. His most famous works included *On the Dignity of Man* and *Heptaplus*. In response to the overt Christianising message of Pico, **Judah Abravanel** published his *Dialoghi d'amore*, which makes the **Torah** of **Moses** the font of all subsequent wisdom. Philosophically, whereas Pico differentiated cosmic from sensual love, Judah tried to show how they were intimately connected to one another.

See **Abravanel, Judah; Alemanno, Yohanan; conversion; Ficino, Marsilio; kabbalah; Platonism**

Plaskow, Judith (b. 1947) is a contemporary Jewish theologian and at the forefront of an emerging discourse known as feminist Jewish philosophy. For Plaskow, the greatest challenge facing contemporary Judaism is the historical and systematic exclusion of women from the activity of biblical interpretation. So even though women were present at **Sinai**, patriarchal structures have silenced women's voices. In her *Standing again at Sinai*, Plaskow calls on Jewish women to begin the process of struggling with the sources of Judaism so that women can take up their rightful place in the tradition of interpreting the Bible. Unlike some other Jewish feminists, Plaskow encourages Jewish women to be not just religiously but also philosophically literate so that they can engage in a creative reading of the tradition that is at the same time philosophically rigorous.

See **commentary; hermeneutics; midrash; Torah**

Platonism: Medieval Platonism is characterised by intellectualism in cognition, the notion that extra-mental ideas are the objects of knowledge, soul–body dualism and the idea that self-knowledge leads to cosmic knowledge. Most medieval Islamic and Jewish thinkers did not have ready access to Plato's dialogues (in fact, it seems that most did not even know that Plato wrote dialogues), rather they encountered the thought of Plato through various summaries and commentaries written by Platonists of late antiquity, in addition to pseudipigraphic sayings attributed to Socrates. Because of this, the thought of Plato was often filtered through Neoplatonic lenses. As a consequence, very few medieval philosophers would have considered themselves 'Platonists'.

The earliest Jewish Platonist is **Philo of Alexandria,** who distinguishes between the unchanging world of the forms (which is perceptible only by the intellect) and the changing material world (perceptible through the senses). Although the main school of thought in the Middle Ages was **Aristotelianism,** the sixteenth century witnessed a renaissance of Plato's teachings, which increasingly offered an alternative to Aristotelian science and **cosmology.** Renaissance Platonists were also interested in using Plato's ideas to explore more deeply concepts such as love, magic and music.

See **Abravanel, Judah; Alemanno, Yohanan; Aristotelianism; cosmology; creation; emanation; Ficino, Marsilio; form; God, knowledge of; God, nature of; happiness; intellect; matter; metaphysics; Neoplatonism; Pico della Mirandola, Giovanni; Plotinus; Theology of Aristotle**

Further reading: Brague 2003; Goodman 1992; Gutas 1998; Melamed 2003; Nasr 1993; Samuelson 1994; Winston 1985; H. A. Wolfson 1972

Plotinus (204–70 CE) is usually regarded as the founder of **Neoplatonism.** He wrote the *Enneads*, part of which circulated in the medieval Judeo-Islamic world as the **Theology of Aristotle,** to which some Islamic philosophers (e.g. **Avicenna**) wrote commentaries. Paradoxically, although no medieval Jewish thinker knew the name of Plotinus, his thought is instrumental in virtually all forms of mysticism, philosophy and theology. This is especially true regarding his **metaphysics,** which posited the One as the ultimate cause of everything in the universe. From the One, there emanates two 'hypostases': **Intellect** (whose thoughts are the Platonic forms) and **Soul** (which produces the sensible world). All individual souls partake of this universal Soul and desire to return to it through the study of philosophy. Since the rational soul is a member of the celestial world it survives the death of the body. There also exists a strong mystical strain in the thought of Plotinus, and he often speaks of the mystical and visual component of the soul's reabsorption back into the world soul.

See emanation; God, knowledge of; God, love of; God, nature of; happiness; intellect; Neoplatonism; Platonism; rational mysticism; soul; Theology of Aristotle

Further reading: Goodman 1992; Gutas 1998; Hughes 2004a; Tanenbaum 2002; E. R. Wolfson 1994

political philosophy: The interest in political philosophy is primarily confined to medieval Jewish philosophers, especially those that came under the influence of **Alfarabi's** writings. The central question that such thinkers addressed is: what are the conditions of the ideal state that permits its inhabitants to attain true **happiness**? Although Islamic philosophers, in particular **ibn Bajja** and **ibn Tufayl,** argue that one can attain true happiness outside of society, virtually all Jewish philosophers agree with Aristotle that 'man is a political animal', and contend that such happiness can only be attained socially. Even though human perfection resides in the individual intellect, one can most easily perfect one's intellect in a just and moral society. In this regard, most agree with **Maimonides,** who posits that the blueprint for the ideal state exists in the **Torah** of **Moses.** These medieval Jewish philosophers, then, are not interested in politics from a theoretical perspective, but in showing how Mosaic Law represents the ideal expression of any political law. As a result one of the primary functions of the prophet is political, since the prophet must share his own intellectual perfection with others by translating rational truths into a language that all can understand.

See **Alfarabi; allegoresis; ethics; halakhah; happiness; Ibn Bajja; Ibn Tufayl; imagination; Maimonides, Moses; metaphor; parables; prophecy; religion; rhetoric; Torah**

Further reading: Black 1990; Fakhry 1983; Frank and Leaman 1997 and 2003; Green 1993; Kraemer

1991; Kreisel 1999 and 2001; Leaman and Nasr 1996; Melamed 2003

Polleqar, Isaac (d. c. 1330) was a close friend of **Abner of Burgos** before his conversion to Christianity, and became one of the first Jewish philosophers to respond to Abner's subsequent attacks on Judaism. He composed commentaries to numerous biblical books, a translation and **commentary** to **Alghazali**'s *Intentions of the Philosophers*, and an independent treatise entitled *Support of the Faith* (*Ezer ha-Dat*), which alone is extant.

This last treatise is not only a refutation of Abner's criticisms but also a very rich and highly literary text that justifies a rational interpretation of Judaism, and is directed against five primary opponents of such interpretation: the ignorant, the sceptical, the astrologers and other believers in strict **determinism**, the non-believers and the kabbalists. The keys to Judaism's superiority, according to Polleqar, are **Moses** and the **Torah**. Polleqar understands Moses in light of **Alfarabi**'s criteria for the king of the virtuous city (e.g. perfect of body, intellect and imagination). The Torah is the perfect teaching because it insures moral, legal and intellectual perfection of those who believe in it. Polleqar is also quick to demonstrate that religion and philosophy need each other and, rather than contradict one other, actually have a complementary relationship. Furthermore, he argues that one should not put a philosophical straightjacket on religion, but rather one should know when and how to apply rational principles to the Torah. He is also extremely critical of astrology (something to which Abner appealed to justify his conversion) and reinforces **Maimonides**' critique of this science.

See **Abner of Burgos; Albalag; Alfarabi; Alghazali; apologetics; astrology; commentary; determinism; free** will; kabbalah; Maimonidean controversies; Maimonides, Moses; Moses; Torah

Further reading: Frank and Leaman 1997; Tirosh-Samuelson 2003

Post-Modernism: Post-Modernism is an extremely difficult concept to define. Most agree that it is a critique of the rationalist **Enlightenment** project, and that it refers to a drastic rethinking of the founding assumptions of western civilisation, everything from the relationship between subject and object to the construction of identity. In terms of religion, Post-Modernist thought tends to negate **metaphysics** or anything else that posits the existence of any objective thought about God or **nature**. Moreover, language no longer becomes referential to things in the world, but reflexive to those who employ language. Post-Modernist **theology**, thus, tries to think about God in ways that are not dependant upon metaphysical assumptions. Such ways can include new versions of **negative theology**, which stress scepticism but tend not to construct God as a supra-essential being (as some of the medieval thinkers did).

See **Heidegger, Martin; hermeneutics; Levinas, Emmanuel; negative theology**

Further reading: Cohen 1994; Gordon 2003

prayer: A central component of Jewish worship. The main philosophical question concerning prayer is: if human perfection and happiness reside in the **intellect,** what role does prayer play in this? If one has attained a certain level of perfection, does one need to engage in worship? Or, is prayer a social convention, geared for those that are unable to attain intellectual perfection on their own?

Speaking generally, most Jewish philosophers are interested in prayer in terms of the proper intention behind it, and making sure that it is directed towards an appropriate understanding of God. Likewise, most are interested only in the human cognitive activity of prayer, not whether God can actually hear such prayer. **Bachya ibn Pakuda**, for instance, argues that all duties of the heart are derived from God's oneness, and only through humility and constant self-examination can the worshipper attain a proper level of purity and truly love God. **Maimonides** also stresses the importance of proper intent in prayer, although he connects prayer to his ideal of contemplative activity. In the act of prayer, in other words, the informed individual contemplates the **divine attributes**. Such an approach to prayer was criticised by individuals such as **Judah Halevi**, who contends that prayer has to be rooted in the particularities of the **Jewish people**, and not any form of intellectual perfection.

In modern Jewish philosophy, **Martin Buber** locates the origin of religion in prayer, which he defines as the encounter between God and another person. Like his medieval precursors, Buber argues that prayer must be understood properly or else it deteriorates into ritual and ultimately idolatry. For **Rosenzweig**, prayer is what unites the three main elements of his thought: God, world and humans. Prayer brings about redemption, which he understands as an orientation towards the world predicated on the notion of love of one's neighbour.

See **chosenness; covenant; divine attributes; ethics; God, knowledge of; God, love of; Halevi, Judah; happiness; Ibn Pakuda, Bachya; Jewish people; Maimonidean controversies; Maimonides, Moses**

prophecy: As with most biblical concepts, there are essentially two competing conceptions of prophecy: the natural and the supernatural. For the great majority of philosophers, prophecy has to be explicable by the same categories used to explain all cognitive activities.

Jewish Aristotelians argue that when the human intellect reaches a certain degree of perfection, through a mastery of the various sciences, it unites with the **Active Intellect**. This is a natural process, in which God becomes only an indirect or remote cause. According to **Maimonides**, the union of the human intellect and Active Intellect creates an overflow into the former and, in some individuals, this leads to a further overflow into the imaginative faculty. So, although every philosopher is not a prophet, every prophet is ultimately a philosopher. Despite this, Maimonides singles out the uniqueness of **Moses' prophecy**, which produced the **Torah**, as being different in kind and not just degree from that of the other prophets. Whereas other prophets relied on their imaginative faculties, Moses did not. Although Moses did not prophesy with his **imagination,** he did use this faculty in communicating information to the masses. Since the Aristotelian position on the quiddity of prophecy was natural, it also naturalised the miraculous.

Jewish thinkers critical of Aristotelianism offer a different paradigm of prophecy, one that tends to emphasise the supernatural component. **Saadia Gaon,** for instance, posits that the prophet is someone who is chosen by God, and someone who can perform **miracles** (although they cannot subvert the rational). In so doing, Saadia claims that prophecy is the creation of a semi-divine entity that mediates between the prophet and God. Similarly, **Judah Halevi** argues that prophecy is a gift that God bestows upon the prophet. Whereas Maimonides and other rationalists tend to downplay the visionary quality of prophecy by reducing it to the oneiric and the imaginative, Halevi argues that the prophets have actual visions that are tantamount to a spiritual reality that God creates for the prophet. Jews in general and prophets in particular, according to this theory, possess an internal faculty that enables them to see phenomena in a non-physical sense.

In modern Jewish philosophy, **Buber** seems to be the most interested in prophecy and he regards this as the encounter between God and an individual, in which the individual subsequently encounters other individuals and thereby draws them into communal worship. Whenever a religion is in danger of deteriorating into mere ritual, prophets (e.g. the founder of Hasidism) arise to renew the tradition. **Heschel**, however, argues that the God of the Bible is a passionate God, whose intimate care for the world manifests itself through prophecy.

See **Abravanel, Isaac; Active Intellect; afterlife; angels; apologetics; Aristotelianism; belief; Buber, Martin; commandments; cosmology; creation; dogma; epistemology; Gersonides; God, nature of; Halevi, Judah; happiness; imagination; intellect; Maimonidean controversies; Maimonides, Moses; Moses; Neoplatonism; religion; religious experience; revelation; rhetoric; Saadia Gaon; Sinai; soul; Torah**

Further reading: Friedman 2002; Kreisel 2001; Reines 1970

providence: Divine providence refers to God's care of, provision for, and direction of the world. Everything in the world, then, somehow fulfills God's purpose. In its most clichéd form, the problem of providence is expressed in the phrase: 'Why do bad things happen to good people'? Theories of providence run the gamut from strong **determinism** that stresses God's absolute control over everything to positions that limit God's knowledge, especially of the future, in order to protect human **free will**. To support the last position, some philosophers go so far as to argue that God cannot know particulars, for the knowledge of anything that changes (i.e. anything composed of **matter**), would imply that there would be a change in God's essence. **Maimonides** responds to this by claiming that God can know individuals, but that he does so with an unchanging knowledge that comes not from the objects of knowledge but from a knowledge that is identical to the divine essence. As a result individual providence can occur when an individual perfects his rational faculty. The reason for this is that the person with a perfected intellect receives some of the emanation coming from the **Active Intellect**, which enables that person to avoid corporeal evils.

Gersonides also equates individual providence with intellectual perfection; however, he also talks about general and inherited providence. General providence is that which bequeaths guidance to the world through the motion of the celestial spheres. Inherited providence is that which can pass from one generation to another. Gersonides uses this type of providence to explain the covenantal relationship between God and the **Jewish people**.

The other Jewish thinker to deal with providence was **Moses Mendelssohn**, who argues, following Leibniz, that this world is 'the best of all possible worlds', and that punishment and reward will be meted out in the **afterlife** since individual identity remains with the soul after physical death.

See **Active Intellect; compatibilism and incompatibilism; determinism; divine will; evil, problem of; free will; Gersonides; God, knowledge of; God, nature of; Ibn Daud, Abraham; intellect; Jewish people; Maimonidean controversies; Maimonides, Moses; matter; Mendelssohn, Moses; monotheism; Nahmanides; omnipotence; omniscience; Shoah, the**

Further reading: Brague 2003; Eisen 1995; Feldman 2003; Harvey 1998; Kellner 1991; Leaman 1997

R

rational mysticism: Mysticism of a rational variety is neither ecstatic nor spontaneous. On the contrary, it is a form of experience that arises after the individual has mastered all of the various sciences associated with the philosophic life. Virtually all of the Jewish philosophers subscribe, in one way or another, to a position that holds rational (or, alternatively, intellectual) mysticism as the *telos* of the intellectual life. This type of mysticism, then, is not to be confused with Sufism ('Islamic mysticism') or **kabbalah;** rather, it has precedents in the philosophical sources of late antiquity.

Philo, for example, argues that the goal of human life is to become God-like, something that culminates in the mystical experience of seeing God. **Neoplatonism,** in general, is not just a discursive or scientific system, but a way of life that aims at the intellectual and religious perfection of the individual.

In Jewish Neoplatonic texts, the goal of the philosophical journey is the return and reabsorption of the human **soul** into the Universal Soul. The desire of the human soul to return to its 'home' is often described using very sensual, poetic language, and the actual reunion is described in highly visual terms. Even **Maimonides,** in certain chapters of the *Guide* (e.g. III: 51) intimates that the worship of the ideal person is 'like' the individual who basks in the presence of his king.

Likewise, **Spinoza,** in the final part of his *Ethics,* argues for the eternity of the mind, immortality of the soul, and the intellectual love of God that is based on intuitive apprehension. For **Buber,** the I–Thou relationship is one that is ultimately predicated on the transformative nature that the individual must undergo, and through this relationship one encounters the presence of God. Even the acceptance of the **commandments**, according to Buber, is contingent upon the dialogue between the individual and God. Similarly, **Rosenzweig** maintains that reality is the matter of the dynamic interaction between humans, God and the world – an interaction that is dependent upon **revelation**, an act that not only occurred in the past but also represents the individual's apprehension that he or she is created and loved by God.

See **Active Intellect; Buber, Martin; God, love of; happiness; Ibn Gabirol, Shlomo; Ibn Pakuda, Bachya; imagination; kabbalah; Maimonides, Moses; Neoplatonism; Philo of Alexandria; religious experience; Rosenzweig, Franz; Spinoza, Baruch; Theology of Aristotle**

Further reading: Friedman 2002; Hughes 2004a; Lobel 2000; Tanenbaum 2002; E. R. Wolfson 1994

reason: For the medieval Jewish philosophers, reason is the defining element of what it means to be a human. The rational faculty is what enables the individual to discern **truth** and thereby to approach God. So even though God revealed the **Torah,** reason is all that humans have at their disposal to access it.

Following Aristotle, most tend to differentiate between practical and theoretical reason. Practical reason consists of knowledge of things that can be otherwise than they are. It is primarily concerned with politics and **ethics** and the ability to make intelligent decisions based on general principles and the ability to formulate how such principles relate to specific situations. Theoretical reason, in contrast, is concerned with the knowledge about that which cannot be otherwise than it is. Theoretical reason, then, is about contemplating unchanging and eternal objects. Since humans are composed of both body and intellect, most of the medieval philosophers argued that the Torah seeks to establish the perfection of both, with perfection of the body corresponding to practical reason and that of the intellect corresponding to theoretical reason.

It is through the balance between these two types of perfection that many (e.g. **Saadia, Ibn Ezra, Maimonides, Gersonides**) understood and classified the **commandments**. For example, circumcision was necessary for dulling the sexual appetite so that the Jewish male could control it. **Moses Mendelssohn** argues that reason (as opposed to **revelation** or **miracles**) is what enables every individual to discern the truths of natural religion (e.g. God is One, God governs the world, immortality of the soul).

According to **Kant**, ethics must be based not on revelation but on reason, and it is in response to this that thinkers such as **Cohen** and **Buber** argue that revelation is tantamount to the establishment of reason.

See **Aristotelianism; autonomy; belief; Cohen, Hermann; commandments; epistemology; ethics; free will; God, knowledge of; God, nature of; halakhah; happiness; immortality; intellect; Maimonides, Moses; matter; Mendelssohn, Moses; metaphysics; Platonism; prophecy; rational mysticism; sin; Torah**

Further reading: Altmann 1973; Cohen 1994; Feiner 2002; Feldman 2003; Seeskin 2001; Tirosh-Samuelson 2003

religion: The medieval period witnessed a tension between the truths of religion and those of philosophy. Most critics, informed or otherwise, often charged philosophers with heresy and, thus, as opponents of religion, at least as classically or traditionally understood.

Alfarabi is one of the first Islamic philosophers who attempts, with varying degrees of success, to harmonise philosophy and religion. He does this by arguing that religion is nothing other than the rhetorical expression of philosophical truths. Philosophy is thus prior in time to religion. Since the prophet was a philosopher with a perfected **imagination**, he was responsible for creating parables and myths (i.e. sacred scriptures) that attempt to lead non-philosophers to some modicum of **happiness**. This is also the opinion of **Maimonides**, only for him Judaism is the best religion because it possessed the best legislation: the **Torah** of **Moses**. Maimonides goes further than this, however, by trying to rationalise Judaism by means of his *Mishneh Torah*, a massive legal compendium. Subsequent to Maimonides, and in response to his principles of **belief**, thinkers as diverse as **Crescas**, **Albo** and **Isaac Abravanel** try to establish their own principles of the tradition that constituted who is or is not a believer.

Modern Jewish philosophical conceptions of religion (in particular, Judaism) can be viewed as various responses to the critiques of **Spinoza** and **Kant**. According to **Moses Mendelssohn**, Judaism is a natural religion (i.e. accessible by reason not **revelation**), but one with a revealed legislation (e.g. the **commandments**). According to **Buber**, religion is a product of a pure I–Thou relationship between the prophet and God. This relationship gradually becomes decadent and idolatrous, only to be renewed periodically in particular movements (i.e. early Hasidism) or in each individual. Opposed to this idea is **Joseph Soloveitchik**, who contends that religion is not individual or a-legal, but is to be found in the very heart of **halakhah** and its observance.

See **Albo, Joseph; Alfarabi; allegory; apologetics; belief; Buber, Martin; Cohen, Hermann; commandments; covenant; Crescas, Hasdai; dogma; halakhah; Halevi, Judah; Jewish people; Kant, Immanuel; Maimonides, Moses; Mendelssohn, Moses; monotheism;**

Neoplatonism; parables; religious experience; Spinoza, Baruch; Torah

Further reading: Eisen 1995; Gordon 2003; Kellner 1986 and 1991; Kreisel 1999 and 2001; Lawee 2001; Lobel 2000; Myers 2003; Preus 2001; Sorkin 1996

religious experience: Obviously crucial to Judaism, religious experience tends to be downplayed or allegorised by medieval Jewish philosophers. Critics of Jewish philosophy claim that philosophers, in marginalising the importance of history and thus of the particularity of the Jewish people, are unconcerned with the inner experience of Jews. Many Jewish philosophers tend, for instance, to equate **prophecy** with a union between the prophet and the **Active Intellect** rather than on what they would consider to be an amorphous type of experience. In modern Jewish philosophy, especially that associated with **Existentialism**, experience becomes central. With its emphasis on the individual, and his or her authenticity, Existentialists such as **Rosenzweig** argue that the rituals of religion, for example, those surrounding the Sabbath, awaken in the individual an experience of God's **creation** on a weekly basis. **Martin Buber,** in like manner, stresses the religious experience in Hasidism as the centrepiece of Jewish religious experience in the modern world.

See **Active Intellect; apologetics; Buber, Martin; Crescas, Hasdai; Existentialism; God, love of; Halevi, Judah; kabbalah; Kaplan, Mordechai; prayer; prophecy; Rosenzweig, Franz**

Further reading: Gordon 2003; Hughes 2004a; Lobel 2000

religious language: When the Bible speaks of **angels** or God's justice, how are these terms to be understood? Does 'angel' literally mean an angel (e.g. a human-like figure with wings) as most people understand it? If so, how does this term fit with Aristotelian or Kantian philosophy? Since Jewish philosophy is essentially about reading the Bible rationally, understanding and contextualising biblical language becomes central. Yet, the language of the Bible is not that of philosophy: it is often unclear, contradictory and almost always unphilosophical. Because the Bible is the *sine qua non* of Jewish existence, rationalist Jewish thinkers seek to understand it philosophically. In this respect, Jewish philosophers are aided by a well-known rabbinic dictum stating that 'the Torah speaks in the language of humans' (*B. Yevamot* 71a; *Bava Metzia* 31b). Sometimes this language is understood literally: For example, **Halevi** claims that when the Bible says that God is actively involved in the world, he truly is. When, however, someone like **Maimonides** reads this, he contends that God, qua Intellect, is unconcerned with particulars, and that even though the Bible may say 'God', it actually means **Active Intellect**. In like manner, religious language is notoriously ambiguous. The book of **Genesis**, for example, mentions the concept of **creation**, but does not specify what this act means. As a result, various thinkers, working with differing philosophical paradigms, interpret 'creation' in various ways.

See **Active Intellect; afterlife; allegoresis; allegory; angels; commentary; creation; Halevi, Judah; Hebrew; immortality; Maimonides, Moses; metaphor; midrash; Moses; prophecy; Talmud; Torah**

Further reading: Lobel 2000; Tanenbaum 2002; Tirosh-Samuelson 2003; E.R. Wolfson 1994

resurrection of the dead see **afterlife; immortality**

revelation: Every major theistic religion has to posit the concept of God revealing in **history** some part of himself to a community of believers. This revelation not only bridges the gap between God and humanity but also succeeds in showing believers the correct way to form a relationship with God.

Most medieval thinkers discuss revelation under the rubric of **prophecy**; for this reason, comments here will be confined to modern thinkers, who tend to de-historicise revelation and make it equivalent to moral duty. For **Mendelssohn**, true religion cannot be revealed because it is accessible to everyone through reason. What is revealed, however, is a legislation that teaches people how to live well. **Hermann Cohen**, responding to **Kant**'s critique of Judaism's heteronomy, argues that revelation is not a historical event that took place thousands of years ago, but a symbol of God's relationship to humanity. Revelation is, for him, synonymous with the establishment of reason. As a consequence, the product of revelation, the **Torah**, is not a historical document, but a process that enables humans to think and act responsibly on their own. For **Martin Buber**, revelation is a dialogical meeting that takes place in the I–Thou relationship, with every I–Thou encounter being a particular manifestation of the encounter between the self and the eternal Thou. For **Franz Rosenzweig**, revelation is something that also occurs in the present, and it is the act that expresses God's act as love. Revelation, thus, becomes the command issued to all humans to love God and, through God, to love other humans, which, in turn, prepares the groundwork for redemption.

See **autonomy; Buber, Martin; Cohen, Hermann; commandments; ethics; God, knowledge of; God, nature of; Heschel, Abraham Joshua; Kant, Immanuel; Leibowitz, Yeshayahu; Mendelssohn, Moses; prophecy; religion; Rosenzweig, Franz; Sinai; Torah**

Further reading: Cohen 1994; Friedman 2002; Gordon 2003; Kaplan 1996; Kreisel 2001; Reines 1970; Samuelson 2002; Seeskin 2001

rhetoric: The power to persuade. Although Plato tended to equate this with the Sophists, medieval thinkers discussed and commented on Aristotle's *Rhetoric* within the context of **logic**. As a result, the focus was on the linguistic and cognitive issues involved in poetic language. A rhetorical syllogism was one that, like its more demonstrative counterpart, depended on a conclusion following logically from premises. And even though a rhetorical syllogism did not create strict analytical assent in the listener, it nonetheless was able to persuade him or her. Islamic philosophers discussed rhetorical syllogisms within the context of a prophet's ability to persuade those unlearned in philosophy. In Muslim Spain, Jewish thinkers (especially, Moses ibn Ezra) used rhetoric to show how the Bible, and by extension Judaism, was superior to Islam. In the Renaissance, rhetoric was considered to be one of the defining characteristics of the *homo universalis* ('universal man'). **Judah Messer Leon** wrote his *Book of the Honeycomb's Flow* to show how the Torah best represents the Renaissance ideal of linguistic eloquence.

See **Abravanel, Judah; aesthetics; apologetics; commentary; logic; Messer Leon, Judah; Neoplatonism**

Further reading: Black 1990; Hughes 2004a and 2004b; Tanenbaum 2002

Rosenzweig, Franz (1886–1929) is one of the greatest Jewish philosophers in the modern period. Although a student of **Hermann Cohen**, Rosenzweig rejected his notion that Judaism was a religion of reason and, thus, simply a particular representation of universal truths. In like manner, he is also critical of German **Idealism,** which he argued took no interest in the individual. Instead, Rosenzweig calls for a 'New Thinking' that will begin not with ideas or thought, but with individual experiences.

Although he composed over forty works, his magnum opus is the *Star of Redemption* (*Der Stern der Erlosung*), a very complex work that is interested in the interaction between God, humans and the world, on the one hand, and **creation, revelation** and redemption on the other. (These six phenomena represent the six points of the Star of David.) The first triad – that between God, humans and the world – Rosenzweig calls 'elements', which are the substances that establish reality; the other three are called 'courses' that show how the various substances relate to one another. Revelation is what connects humans and God; creation that which connects God and the world; and redemption that which connects humans and the world. Within this context or star, Judaism offers the path to meaning and authenticity in the world. For Rosenzweig, Judaism is not a historical religion (unlike Christianity, which is), but its rituals, myths and liturgy enable Jews to establish a living relationship with God, something that no other religion can do. For this reason, Rosenzweig was opposed to **Zionism,** which, for him, was the attempt to get Jews to reenter **history.** To do this would be tantamount to destroying the unity between God, humans and the world, which already existed in the heart of Judaism.

See **anti-Semitism; Buber, Martin; Cohen, Hermann; covenant; God, nature of; Halevi, Judah; Hegel, Georg Wilhelm Friedrich; Heidegger, Martin; Idealism; Jewish people; nature; revelation; religious experience**

Further reading: Batnitzky 2000; Cohen 1994; Frank and Leaman 1997; Gordon 2003; Mack 2003; Myers 2003; Samuelson 1989 and 1994

S

Saadia Gaon (882–942) was one of the earliest rationalists in medieval Judaism. He was head of the Rabbinic Academy located at Sura (Babylonia), was in correspondence with **Isaac Israeli**, and was a vociferous critic of the **Karaites** and their denial of rabbinic authority. He was also a biblical exegete, translator of the Bible into Arabic, grammarian and liturgist. His most important philosophical work is the *Book of Beliefs and Opinions* (*Sefer Emunot ve-De'ot*, originally written in Arabic as *Kitab al-Amanat wa al-i'tiqadat*), which demonstrates the rationality of rabbinic Judaism and which is directed against two main opponents: Karaites and rationalists who deny the **Torah**.

At the beginning of this work, Saadia argues that there are three primary sources of knowledge: sense perception, reason (e.g. the whole is bigger than its parts) and logical inference (e.g. where there is smoke, there is fire). In addition to these three, the **Jewish people** are unique in having a fourth source: the reliability of tradition. The work proper is divided into ten treatises, and relies heavily on both the structure and the rational-theological argumentation of texts written by the **Mutazilites**. For example, after establishing that the world was created *ex nihilo*, he discusses God's unity and justice (two hallmarks of the Mutazilites).

In response to Karaite claims, Saadia argues that anthropomorphic expressions in the Bible must be understood metaphorically (e.g. 'hand' denotes power), and that the **halakhah** was given to the Jews so that they could live well and attain **happiness**. Saadia divides the **commandments** into two categories: those of reason (e.g. prohibition against murder and adultery) and those of revelation (e.g. dietary laws, Sabbath, holy days). Saadia also developed the concept of the 'second air' (as opposed to 'normal' air), which functions as an audible and visible intermediary between God and the prophet during the act of **prophecy**. Although Saadia framed all of the main issues of subsequent Jewish philosophy, many tended to look back at him as more of a theologian than a philosopher.

See **afterlife; apologetics; Asharites; commandments; creation; divine attributes; God, arguments for the existence of; God, knowledge of; God, nature of; happiness; Israeli, Isaac; Jewish people; kalam; Karaites; miracles; Mutazilites; prophecy; religious language; Talmud; Torah**

Further reading: Frank and Leaman 1997 and 2003; Guttmann 1964; Sirat 1985; Tirosh-Samuelson 2003

Scholasticism: The philosophical-theological teaching and methods that arose in medieval Christendom. Philosophically, it represents the incorporation of Aristotelian principles to articulate Christian teaching. Although originally denounced as heretical, Scholasticism eventually became the official system of thought of the Catholic Church. Scholasticism gradually became associated with the main curricula of European universities. Jewish philosophers increasingly came under the influence of Scholasticism in the late fourteenth century. The scholastic method of argumentation – the inclusion of a summary of an issue, the presentation of pro and con arguments, and the subsequent rebuttal of the objections – was incorporated into the composition of Jewish philosophical texts (e.g. the work of **Isaac Abravanel**).

See **Abner of Burgos; Abravanel, Isaac; Albo, Joseph; Aristotelianism; Crescas, Hasdai; Polleqar, Isaac**

Further reading: Feldman 2003; Frank and Leaman 1997 and 2003; Tirosh-Rothschild 1991

Sefer Yetzirah: The *Sefer Yetzirah* (*The Book of Creation*) was a work of early Jewish cosmological and cosmogonic speculation about the formation of the universe. It was also the work that coined the term *sefirot* to denote various entities created by God (but which later came to designate the divine structure of the universe). Because of its brevity and esoteric style, many early Jewish philosophers (e.g. **Saadia Gaon, Abraham ibn Ezra**) wrote commentaries on the *Sefer Yetzirah* because it offered an authentic **Hebrew** vocabulary and a set of Jewish categories with which to speculate about **cosmology**. Such thinkers also argued that this treatise could not be understood literally, but had to be explained philosophically.

See **Abulafia, Abraham; commentary; cosmology; Ibn Ezra, Abraham; kabbalah; parables; Saadia Gaon**

Further reading: Scholem 1974; E. R. Wolfson 1994

Shoah, the: According to many contemporary Jewish thinkers no event has had a bigger impact on post-World War Two Jewish philosophy and identity than the Shoah (Holocaust). The extermination of European Jewry in the early and middle of the twentieth century has challenged virtually all of Judaism's inherited truths and long-held assumptions, from **God** to the **chosenness** of the **Jewish people** to the meaning of **history**. In many ways, the Shoah is a unique event and, as a result, numerous thinkers, both Jewish and Christian, have struggled to make philosophical sense of it. Some have contended that the only way to comprehend a place like Auschwitz and to protect human **free will** is through silence. Likewise, **Martin Buber** claims that the Shoah represents an eclipse of God. The Shoah is thus intimately connected to the age-old problem of **free will** versus **determinism**. How could God let something like this happen to his covenantal partners? I. Maybaum has argued that God used Hitler in the same way that he used Pharoah or Nebuchadnezzar. Such a position, many criticise, does little to understand the carnage or suffering.

In contradistinction, Arthur Cohen has tried to redefine the very **nature of God** so that he is not responsible for the particular events of history and thus cannot be held responsible for acts of human **evil**. Another, more severe, approach is offered by Richard Rubenstein, who has reasoned that:

1. God could not have allowed the Shoah to happen.
2. The Shoah did happen.
3. Therefore, God does not exist.

Yet, rather than call for the dismantling of Judaism, Rubenstein argues that the key to Jewish renewal resides in the natural (as opposed to the historical) world. Others claim that the Shoah represents the shattering of the traditional **covenant** between God and Israel, and that the post-Shoah period must witness a new covenantal relationship, variously defined, between the two.

Mention should also be made of other perspectives on the Shoah. Some contend that this event is neither more nor less unique than other national tragedies (e.g. destruction of the Temple, exile from Spain). **Yeshayahu Leibowitz**, for example, posits that the Shoah, as a historical event, has no independent value, something that can only come about through a relationship to the **commandments**.

See **anti-Semitism; autonomy; Buber, Martin; chosenness; covenant; determinism; evil, problem of; free will; God, arguments for the existence of; God, nature of; history; Israel, state of; Levinas, Emmanuel; Post-Modernism; providence; Zionism**

Further reading: Cohen 1994; Frank and Leaman 1997; Friedman 2002; Katz 1992; Leaman 1997; Myers 2003; Samuelson 1989; Seeskin 1990

sin: Since Judaism does not believe in 'original sin', the rabbis understood sin as the failure to observe the divine **commandments;** this failure was the result of the evil impulse 'located in the heart' of every individual. Medieval Neoplatonists locate the capacity for sin in the animal **soul,** which they associate with various desires of the body. Neoplatonic psychology is thus concerned with the ongoing struggle in every individual between the rational soul and the animal instincts.

Maimonides locates the introduction of sin with Adam. According to his reading of the **Genesis** story, Adam was originally engaged in pure intellectual contemplation of God. However, because Adam, based on his own choices, inclined towards his **imagination** and the body, he was forced to engage in practical **reason,** that is, enter the social sphere involving interaction with other humans. For Maimonides, this is an **allegory** for the choices that every human must make: either they can engage in theoretical contemplation located in the **intellect** or they can focus on moral action, which is located in the body.

In modern Jewish philosophy sin is also associated with choices confronting each individual. Sin, for **Hermann Cohen,** is the distance that opens up between the individual and the moral order. The avoidance of sin is associated with the internalisation of the law and, through this, into a meaningful relationship with others and with God.

See **autonomy; Cohen, Hermann; commandments; covenant; ethics; evil, problem of; happiness; intellect; imagination; Maimonides, Moses; Neoplatonism; parables; reason; soul**

Further reading: Batnitzky 2000; Goodman 1992; Kreisel 1999 and 2001; Leaman 1997

Sinai: The mountain that **Moses** ascended to receive the **Torah,** establishing the **covenant** between God and the **Jewish people.** Because Sinai is the formative event in Judaism, Jewish philosophers have interpreted this event according to what they consider to be the essence of **religion.** According to **Philo** it was on Sinai that Moses apprehended the incorporeal world of the Platonic forms. Although Moses was a prophet, most medieval thinkers were adamant in positing that his **prophecy** was unique. According to **Abraham ibn Ezra,** for example, on Sinai Moses was not so much a prophet but a pure **form** that received the revelation directly from God and not through any intermediary. **Judah Halevi,** in contrast, stresses the fact that all of the Israelites experienced the events on Sinai, thus establishing a collective historical experience of the Jewish people.

Maimonides' interpretation of the events at Sinai is somewhere between those of ibn Ezra and Halevi. For him, Moses alone heard all of the revelation clearly but the Israelites heard only the first two commandments (both of which are accessible to reason and not revelation) and witnessed various sounds and sights (which he equated with meteorological phenomena). This is similar to **Moses Mendelssohn's** claim that what was revealed on Sinai was not religion, which is accessible to **reason,** but the commandments, which are not. Modern Jewish philosophers tend to emphasise that Sinai is not so much a historical event, something that took place thousands of years ago, but a symbol for the creation of human reason. This is especially the argument of **Hermann Cohen,** who, following **Kant,** stresses the importance of internal as opposed to external revelation. This internal revelation appeals to human reason and gives the moral law its validity.

See **Active Intellect; allegory; autonomy; Cohen, Hermann; commandments; covenant; God, knowledge of; halakhah; Halevi, Judah; history; Ibn Ezra, Abraham; imagination; intellect; Kant, Immanuel; Karaites; Maimonides, Moses; Mendelssohn, Moses; miracles; Moses; Philo of Alexandria; political philosophy; prophecy; reason; religion; religious experience; revelation; Talmud; Torah**

Further reading: Cohen 1994; Friedman 2002; Gordon 2003; Kaplan 1996; Kreisel 2001; Reines 1970; Samuelson 2002; Seeskin 2001

Soloveitchik, Joseph (1903–93) was primarily a theologian and a halakhist, although his writings do emphasise the individual and his or her relationship to **religion**. The main question that occupies Soloveitchik is the relationship between the individual and God. He contends that the sum and substance of this relationship is through the **Torah** and the **halakhah**.

In his *Halakhic Man*, he claims that this ideal type of individual is not someone so blinded by tradition that he has no place in the modern world, but that he actually represents the values that epitomised modern western culture: intelligence, autonomy, authenticity and creativity. The halakhah, for Soloveitchik, is not a rigid set of rules, but the path towards true human meaning and authenticity on both the bodily and spiritual levels. The halakhah moreover is not followed simply out of duty or habit, but must be worked out – intellectually, emotionally and spiritually – by every individual.

See **Buber, Martin; commandments; Existentialism; God, knowledge of; halakhah; Jewish people; Leibowitz, Yeshayahu; reason; religion; revelation; Talmud; Torah**

Further reading: Frank and Leaman 1997; Leaman 1997

soul: The existence, nature of, and fate of the soul after death were among the central preoccupations of medieval Islamic and Jewish philosophers. Following their Greek predecessors, they argue that the soul is composed of both rational (the rational soul) and irrational (vegetative and animal souls) parts. Although the irrational parts of the soul are tied to the body and ultimately perish with its death, the rational soul, in which is located the **intellect**, is the essence of humans and is considered immortal. The goal of life is to get the rational soul to engage in theoretical sciences so that it can contemplate eternal intelligibles, which are perceived to be equivalent to human **happiness**. The central philosophical question concerning the immortal soul is how it can retain its individuality after the death of the body, which functions as the basis of particularity.

There did exist, however, a debate as to the actual fate of the soul after death. Some (e.g. **Alfarabi**, perhaps **Maimonides, Averroes**) argue that the rational soul, if it is eternal, has no individuality after corporeal death; others (e.g. **Shlomo ibn Gabirol, Abraham bar Hiyya, Abraham ibn Ezra**) contend that the soul preexists the body and is immortal, although they are often unclear if this immortal soul retains its individuality; still others (e.g. **Avicenna**) hold that the soul was created with the body, yet was immortal. According to **Gersonides** the rational soul is immortal and does retain its individuality after bodily death based on the specific intelligibles that each intellect has acquired during its lifetime. **Moses Mendelssohn**, following Leibniz, argued that this is the 'best of all possible worlds' and, because this is based on the nature of God's goodness, the soul must retain its individuality after death.

See **Active Intellect**; afterlife; **Alfarabi**; Alexander of Aphrodisias; **Averroes**; **Avicenna**; **Bar Hiyya, Abraham**; emanation; God knowledge of; God, nature of; happiness; **Ibn Ezra, Abraham**; **Ibn Gabirol, Shlomo**; immortality; imagination; intellect; matter; **Neoplatonism**; **Plotinus**

Further reading: Brague 2003; Goodman 1992; Hughes 2004a; Tanenbaum 2002

Spinoza, Baruch (1632–77) is one of the most important thinkers in the history of philosophy. He received a traditional Jewish education and was familiar with the writings of the medieval Jewish philosophers (e.g. **Maimonides, Crescas**). On 27 July 1656, Spinoza was excommunicated from the Jewish community of Amsterdam for his 'wicked ways' and 'abominable heresies'. He neither converted to Christianity nor did he seek subsequent reinstatement in the Jewish community. Although he published a number of treatises, his two most important ones are the *Theological-Political Treatise* (published anonymously) and the *Ethics* (only published after his death because of its radical doctrines).

In the *Ethics*, Spinoza equates God with **nature** (*Deus, sive Natura*), which for him is equivalent to the rational order pervading the universe. This order can be grasped fully by the human mind only by rigorous methodology grounded in mathematics, and the knowledge of this order represents true human **happiness**. Spinoza, thus, defines God in a way that is completely different from either classical Judaism or classical Jewish philosophy. However, he does argue in the closing sections of the *Ethics* that the intellectual love of God is the highest human perfection.

His *Theological-Political Treatise* is a plea for freedom of thought and religious toleration. Much of this plea takes the form of a systematic critique of the Bible in order to challenge its claim to any sort of authority by those who claim that it is the revealed word of God and that they alone have the right to interpret it. (Indeed, some locate in this critique the origins of modern, secular biblical criticism.) Spinoza's hermeneutical strategy is not to read into the text something that is not there. He is, thus, very critical of **Maimonides**' attempt to make the Bible into a rational text that is expressed allegorically or parabolically. He argues that prophets are not philosophers, but individuals with good imaginations (but not necessarily good intellects), and that **miracles** were natural occurrences that were misunderstood by those present and then erroneously passed down to later generations. Although Spinoza praises the moral teachings of the Bible, he is adamantly opposed to those who would claim any sort of spiritual authority because they somehow have access to biblical 'truths'. **Hermann Cohen** was extremely critical of Spinoza, accusing him of misreading both the Bible and Judaism.

See **ethics; God, knowledge of; God, love of; God, nature of; nature; pantheism; Torah**

Further reading: Frank and Leaman 1997; Guttmann 1964; Kreisel 2001; Preus 2001; Samuelson 1989; Smith 1997 and 2003; H. A. Wolfson 1934

Strauss, Leo (1899–1973) was a leading political philosopher in Germany and later the US, and was largely responsible for the renaissance of **Maimonides** in the twentieth century. He is frequently depicted as a critic of the advances of liberalism, and the preserver of a tradition grounded in natural rights, which have historically been appreciated by a select group of thinkers. These thinkers often had to disguise their true ideas by writing esoterically to the select few, and by hiding their true ideas from the various religious and political forces of the day (hence, his famous book called *Persecution and the Art of Writing*).

Of particular importance for Strauss is the thought of Maimonides. Maimonides, he claims, was a true citizen of Athens (i.e. a philosopher) as opposed to a citizen of Jerusalem (i.e. a religious thinker). Despite this, Maimonides was forced to write in such a manner that obfuscated his true ideas (see, e.g., Strauss's 'How to Begin to Study the *Guide of the Perplexed*'). In his reading of Maimonides, Strauss is extremely critical of his contemporary **Julius Guttmann**, who he accuses of historicising Maimonides and, therefore, misreading his contribution to subsequent Jewish thought. For the full details of Strauss's critique, see his *Philosophie und Gesetz*, translated into English as *Philosophy and Law*. In the modern period, Strauss is regarded as an important thinker in American neo-conservative politics.

See **Guttmann, Julius; Maimonides, Moses; Wissenschaft des Judentums**

Further reading: Green 1993

Talmud: As part of the oral **Torah**, the Talmud is also an important source for Jewish philosophy. The Babylonian Talmud was redacted in the seventh century CE; in the medieval period, both **Karaites** and Christians ridiculed it for its various anthropomorphisms. In 1239 and 1244 it was publicly burned by the Catholic Church because of its perceived blaspheming of Christianity. **Maimonides** argues that the rabbis, whose words are archived in the Talmud, were philosophers who revealed the truth only to those who could properly understand it. In the *Guide*,

Maimonides shows the philosophical truths that exist in the parables and stories told by the rabbis. In addition, in his *Mishneh Torah*, Maimonides essentially rationalises both the content and mode of presentation of the Talmud and other rabbinic legal texts.

The role of the Talmud in modern Jewish philosophy is perhaps best witnessed in the debate between **Buber** and **Rosenzweig**. Buber is ambivalent towards the **halakhah** (the main source of which is the Talmud) because he is suspicious of its intricate system of laws that, for him, can marginalise the authentic relationship that the individual should have with God. **Rosenzweig**, in contrast, argues that the halakhah is the ideal system where the Jew encounters God and explores his relationship to him. Siding with Rosenzweig, **Joseph Soloveitchik** claims that halakhah is not restrictive but liberating, allowing the individual to truly realise his or her spiritual and bodily existences.

See **allegoresis; allegory; anti-Semitism; Buber, Martin; commandments; covenant; God, knowledge of; God, love of; halakhah; Maimonides, Moses; metaphor; parables; religion; Torah**

Themistius (c. 317–c. 388 CE) was an important philosopher of late antiquity who wrote commentaries and summaries of the Aristotelian corpus. His most important work for medieval Jewish philosophy was his paraphrase of Aristotle's *De anima*. In this work, he interpreted Aristotle as arguing for intellect as a separate substance (as opposed to **Alexander of Aphrodisias**, who argued that the intellect was only a disposition to intellectualise). Themistius was also instrumental in locating the **Active Intellect** as a semi-divine intellect (a 'second god') responsible for activating individual potential intellects in the sublunar world. The human intellect that conjoins with this Active Intellect, according to Themistius, becomes immortal.

See **Active Intellect**; afterlife; **Alexander of Aphrodisias**; **Aristotelianism**; **Avicenna**; emanation; epistemology; **God, nature of**; happiness; immortality; intellect; matter; **Neoplatonism**; prophecy; **Theology of Aristotle**

theodicy: If God is unable to prevent **evil**, then he must not be omnipotent; if he is unwilling to prevent it, then he must not be benevolent; if he does not know that evil exists, then he must not be omniscient. Not surprisingly, then, the problem of theodicy is of central concern to Jewish philosophers. There are several solutions: one is to argue that God's justice will insure that at some later time (usually in the next world) the guilty will be punished and the innocent rewarded (e.g. **Saadia Gaon** and most Neoplatonists); a second solution is that the evil has nothing whatsoever to do with God because it is simply a privation of good that is an essential characteristic of **matter** (e.g. **Maimonides** and most Aristotelians); another solution is that of transmigration of souls (e.g. **Nahmanides** and others associated with the **kabbalah**).

In the modern period, theodicy is most closely associated with discussions of the **Shoah**. **Martin Buber**, for example, argued for the 'eclipse of God', which stressed the suffering of the innocent and made no room for any theodicy. Others, for example, Arthur Cohen, have argued that theodicy is no longer important and that God is indifferent to the problem of evil and human suffering.

See **belief**; **chosenness**; **determinism**; **divine attributes**; **divine will**; **evil, problem of**; **God, knowledge of**; **God, nature of**; **history**; **matter**

Further reading: Frank and Leaman 1997; Friedman 2002; Katz 1992; Leaman 1997; Samuelson 1989; Seeskin 1990

theology: Broadly defined, theology is the defence of one's religious tradition based on rational arguments. Although one could make the case that virtually all Jewish philosophers are, on one level, theologians, many (especially in the medieval period) did not consider themselves as such. **Maimonides,** for example, is extremely critical of **kalam** and faults its practitioners for finding premises to back up their already established conclusions. The classic example of a practitioner of medieval Jewish theology is **Saadia Gaon,** who uses the methods and arguments of the **Mutazilites** to defend rationally virtually all of the major tenets of rabbinic Judaism. Other examples would be critics of philosophy (e.g. **Judah Halevi, Hasdai Crescas, Isaac Abravanel**) who use philosophical method to undermine the philosophers and argue rationally for more traditional theological concepts (e.g. **miracles, prophecy**).

In the modern period, the border separating philosophy and theology is perhaps even more fluid. For example, **Martin Buber**'s later work on the Bible emphasises both the I–Thou encounter in the text and the Bible's narrative as providing the basic framework for Jews to understand and contextualise their experiences, both individually and collectively. With his 'New Thinking', **Rosenzweig** attempts to free his work from traditional theological categories (e.g. eternity) while still making room for theology within the context of human life.

See **Abravanel, Isaac; apologetics; Asharites; commandments; Crescas, Hasdai; dogma; God, arguments for the existence of; halakhah; Halevi, Judah; kalam; Mutazilites; political philosophy; religion; religious experience; Talmud; theodicy; Torah**

Theology of Aristotle: The *Theology of Aristotle* was a work that circulated in the medieval Islamic world. Although it was attributed to Aristotle it was actually a summary of **Plotinus'** *Enneads*, especially the more mystically inclined sections of the work. Since it was attributed to

Aristotle, many of the philosophers had to make sense of this work within the context of Aristotle's other works. The result was the 'Neoplatonisation' of Aristotle. The *Theology* was only one of a number of Neoplatonic texts attributed to Plato or Aristotle that circulated in medieval Islam.

See **Aristotelianism; emanation; Neoplatonism; Neopythagoreanism; Platonism; Plotinus; rational mysticism**

Further reading: Gutas 1998; Hughes 2004a; Tanenbaum 2002

theurgy: Literally 'divine-working', theurgy was an important part of some schools of **Neoplatonism,** especially those associated with the teachings of Iamblichus (c. 242–c. 327 CE). Theurgy works on the assumption that certain rituals and practices (e.g. incantations) done by individuals in this world affect the divine world. Theurgy would become an important part of the **kabbalah,** in which every kabbalist was caught up in the attempt to create harmony in the supernal world, and the proper performance of Jewish rituals played an important role in this.

See **Abulafia, Abraham; Alemanno, Yohanan; God, nature of; Hebrew; kabbalah; Neoplatonism**

Further reading: Idel 1989; Scholem 1974

Torah: The Torah occupies the heart of all forms of Judaism (e.g. rabbinic, philosophical, mystical). It is a complex term that has at least three distinct yet overlapping meanings: (1) the five books of **Moses** (i.e. the Pentateuch), (2) the entire Hebrew Bible, and (3) the written Torah and the oral Torah (e.g. **Talmud**).

The Torah is not only the repository of the **commandments,** but also is conceived of as the blueprint of creation. Since the Torah contains many anthropomorphisms and anthropopathisms, these have to be interpreted (e.g. as metaphors). The entire Jewish philosophical enterprise, then, is reading the Torah rationally, using the methods that are adopted and adapted from the larger non-Jewish societies in which Jews found and continue to find themselves. Whereas the **kabbalah** regards it as God's autobiography (in which the mystics play an important role), the medieval philosophers regarded it as divine legislation that, when interpreted properly, creates the ideal state, and, thus, the Torah functions as the perfect prescription for attaining human **happiness**.

In modern Jewish philosophy, the focus is less on the metaphysical and political aspects of the Torah and more on its ethical and moral content, wherein God's relationship to humanity is established.

See **allegoresis**; **commandments**; **covenant**; **God, knowledge of**; **God, nature of**; **halakhah**; **happiness**; **hermeneutics**; **kabbalah**; **political philosophy**; **reason**; **religion**; **Talmud**

transcendence: In traditional Judaism, like other monotheisms, God is considered to be transcendent to the world that he has created. The questions that arise, in both religion and philosophy, are as follows. What is God's relationship to this world? If God is so far removed from this world, how can one have any form of relationship with or experience of him? Is he so above the affairs of this world that he is uninterested in it? Jewish Neoplatonists and Aristotelians attempt to solve this problem through the concept of **emanation**, with the **Active Intellect** functioning as the intermediary between God and the world. This enables thinkers such as **Maimonides** and **Gersonides** to protect God's absolute unity on the one hand and still account for the existence of **prophecy** on the other. Even a critic of philosophy such as **Judah Halevi,** who tries to dismantle the concept of emanated intellects, still posits the existence of the *'amr* ('command', 'word' or 'logos'), which, although more volitional, still mediates between God and the world. The biggest critique of divine transcendence comes from **Spinoza,** who argues that God is immanent in **nature.** Modern Jewish philosophers as diverse as **Cohen, Rosenzweig** and **Levinas** locate transcendence in interpersonal relationships.

See **Active Intellect; Buber, Martin; Cohen, Hermann; cosmology; divine will; emanation; God, nature of; Halevi, Judah; Levinas, Emmanuel; monotheism; Neoplatonism; omnipotence; omniscience; prophecy; Spinoza, Baruch**

Further reading: Brague 2003; Friedman 2002; Kreisel 1999; Leaman 1997; Seeskin 2000

Wissenschaft des Judentums is the scientific study of Judaism, the precursor of the modern discipline of Jewish Studies. By subjecting the religion to the categories (e.g. **historicism,** secular biblical criticism) supplied by the nineteenth-century German academy, those associated with this movement tried to overturn what they perceived to be Judaism's overreliance on 'talmudism' and its non-historical mode of thought. This was not simply an academic exercise, however; at stake for many of these scholars was the very survival and florescence of Judaism in the modern world. Using the methods of modern critical scholarship, Wissenschaft scholars produced a comprehensive literary and historical account of Judaism. Because they stressed the rational aspect of Judaism, they were most interested in Jewish philosophy and were very critical of the 'irrationalism' of **kabbalah**. Many associated with this movement, at least in its earliest stages, were Jewish reformers (e.g. **Abraham Geiger**). Very critical of this approach was **Franz Rosenzweig**, who claims that Judaism does not need history because it existed outside of it.

See **Enlightenment**; **Geiger, Abraham**; **historicism**; **history**; **Krochmal, Nachman**; **Mendelssohn, Moses**; **Zionism**

Further reading: Frank and Leaman 1997; Meyer 1967; Myers 2003; Sorkin 1996

Zionism: The movement that argues that the **Jewish people**, owing to millennia of persecutions, need to have their own nation. Since Jews are always a marginalised minority in the countries where they find themselves they are unable to develop properly as a people, in the ways that other peoples do. Zionism began as a secular enterprise because, in traditional Judaism, it is the Messiah who will be responsible for leading the Jews back to **Israel**.

Historically, Zionism emerges from and is influenced by the idea of nationalism that swept throughout Europe in the nineteenth century. An important philosophical impetus for Zionism was the thought of **Hegel**, which argues that every people has a defining spiritual principle that justifies nations of various peoples. Many (e.g. **Fackenheim, Kaplan**) claim that the formation of the state of Israel would reawaken the Jewish people to their destiny. **Martin Buber** agrees that it is important for Jews to be a holy people in their own land, but it would have to be a country in which Jews and Arabs have complete equality with one another.

Other philosophers are critical of part or all of the Zionist enterprise. **Rosenzweig,** for instance, is opposed to Zionism because it implies that Jews should be just like other peoples (i.e. existing in as opposed to beyond **history).** Leibowitz, in contrast, is not so much critical of Zionism per se, but of secular Zionism that tries to exist without **halakhah.**

See **anti-Semitism; Buber, Martin; chosenness; Enlightenment; Fackenheim, Emil; gentiles; Hegel, Georg Wilhelm Friedrich; Israel, state of; Jewish people; Kaplan, Mordechai; Rosenzweig, Franz**

Further reading: Frank and Leaman 1997; Katz 1992; Samuelson 1989

Selected Bibliography

Altmann, Alexander (1973), *Moses Mendelssohn: A Biographical Study*, Philadelphia: Jewish Publication Society.

Batnitzky, Leora (2000), *Idolatry and Representation: The Philosophy of Franz Rosenzweig Reconsidered*, Princeton, NJ: Princeton University Press.

Black, Deborah L. (1990), *Logic and Aristotle's Rhetoric and Poetics in Medieval Arabic Philosophy*, Leiden: Brill.

Bland, Kalman (2000), *The Artless Jew: Medieval and Modern Affirmations and Denials of the Visual*, Princeton, NJ: Princeton University Press.

Brague, Rémi (2003), *The Wisdom of the World: The Human Experience of the Universe in Western Thought*, translated by Teresa Lavender Fagan, Chicago: University of Chicago Press.

Cohen, Richard A. (1994), *Elevation: The Height of the Good in Rosenzweig and Levinas*, Chicago: University of Chicago Press.

Eisen, Robert (1995), *Gersonides on Providence, Covenant, and the Chosen People: A Study in Medieval Jewish Philosophy and Biblical Commentary*, Albany, NY: State University of New York Press.

Eisen, Robert (2004), *The Book of Job in Medieval Jewish Philosophy*, Oxford: Oxford University Press.

Fakhry, Majid (1983), *A History of Islamic Philosophy*, 2nd edn, New York: Columbia University Press.

Feiner, Shmuel (2002), *The Jewish Enlightenment*, translated by Chaya Naor, Philadelphia, PA: University of Pennsylvania Press.

Feldman, Seymour (2003), *Philosophy in a Time of Crisis: Don Isaac Abravanel, Defender of the Faith*, London: Routledge Curzon.

Frank, Daniel H., and Oliver Leaman (1997), *History of Jewish Philosophy*, New York: Routledge.

Frank, Daniel H., and Oliver Leaman (2003), *The Cambridge Companion to Medieval Jewish Philosophy*, Cambridge: Cambridge University Press.

Frank, Daniel H, Oliver Leaman and Charles H. Manekin (2000), *The Jewish Philosophy Reader*, London: Routledge.

Friedman, Maurice S. (2002), *Martin Buber: The Life of Dialogue*, 4th edn, London: Routledge.

Goodman, Lenn E. (1992), *Neoplatonism and Jewish Thought*, Albany, NY: State University of New York Press.

Gordon, Peter Eli (2003), *Rosenzweig and Heidegger: Between Judaism and German Philosophy*, Berkeley, CA: University of California Press.

Green, Kenneth Hart (1993), *Jew and Philosopher: The Return to Maimonides in the Jewish Thought of Leo Strauss*, Albany, NY: State University of New York Press.

Glazer, Nahum N. (1977), *Modern Jewish Thought: A Source Reader*, New York: Schocken.

Gutas, Dimitri (1998), *Greek Thought, Arabic Culture: The Graeco-Arabic Translation Movement in Baghdad and Early Abbasid Society*, London: Routledge.

Guttmann, Julius (1964), *Philosophies of Judaism: A History of Jewish Philosophy from Biblical Times to Franz Rosenzweig*, New York: Schocken.

Harris, Jay M. (1991), *Nachman Krochmal: Guiding the Perplexed of the Modern Age*, New York: New York University Press.

Harvey, Warren Zev (1998), *Physics and Metaphysics in Hasdai Crescas*, Amsterdam: J. C. Gieben.

Hayoun, Maurice R. (1986), *Moshe Narboni*, Tübingen: J.C.B. Mohr.

Herring, Basil (1982), *Joseph Ibn Kaspi's Gevia Kesef: A Study in Medieval Jewish Philosophic Bible Commentary*, New York: Ktav.

Hughes, Aaron W. (2004a), *The Texture of the Divine: Imagination in Medieval Islamic and Jewish Thought*, Bloomington, IN: Indiana University Press, 2004.

Hughes, Aaron W. (2004b), 'Transforming the Maimonidean Imagination: Aesthetics in the Renaissance Thought of Judah Abravanel', *Harvard Theological Review*, 97.4.

Idel, Moshe (1989), *Language, Torah, and Hermeneutics in Abraham Abulafia*, Albany, NY: State University of New York Press.

Kaplan, Edward K. (1996), *Holiness in Words: Abraham Joshua Heschel's Poetics of Piety*, Albany, NY: State University of New York Press.

Katz, Steven T. (1992), *Historicism, the Holocaust, and Zionism: Critical Studies in Modern Jewish Thought*, New York: New York University Press.

Kellner, Menachem (1986), *Dogma in Medieval Jewish Thought: From Maimonides to Abravanel*, London: Littman Library.

Kellner, Menahem (1991), *Maimonides on Judaism and the Jewish People*, Albany, NY: State University of New York Press.

Kraemer, Joel L. (1991), *Perspectives on Maimonides: Philosophical and Historical Studies*, London: Littman Library.

Kreisel, Howard (1999), *Maimonides' Political Thought: Studies in Ethics, Law, and the Human Ideal*, Albany, NY: State University of New York Press.

Kreisel, Howard (2001), *Prophecy: The History of an Idea in Medieval Jewish Philosophy*, Dordrecht: Kluwer.

Lawee, Eric (2001), *Isaac Abarbanel's Stance toward Tradition: Defense, Dissent, and Dialogue*, Albany, NY: State University of New York Press.

Leaman, Oliver (1997), *Evil and Suffering in Jewish Philosophy*, Cambridge: Cambridge University Press.

Leaman, Oliver, and Seyyed Hossein Nasr (1996), *History of Islamic Philosophy*, London: Routledge.

Lobel, Diana (2000), *Between Mysticism and Philosophy: Sufi Language of Religious Experience in Judah Ha-Levi's Kuzari*, Albany, NY: State University of New York Press.

Mack, Michael (2003), *German Idealism and the Jew: The Inner Anti-Semitism of Philosophy and German Jewish Responses*, Chicago: University of Chicago Press.

Melamed, Abraham (2003), *The Philosopher-King in Medieval and Renaissance Jewish Political Thought*, Albany, NY: State University of New York Press.

Mendes-Flohr, Paul, and Jehuda Reinharz (1995), *The Jew in the Modern World: A Documentary History*, 2nd edn, Oxford: Oxford University Press.

Meyer, Michael A. (1967), *The Origins of the Modern Jew: Jewish Identity and European Culture in Germany, 1749–1824*, Detroit, MI: Wayne State University Press.

Myers, David N. (2003), *Resisting History: Historicism and Its Discontents in German-Jewish Thought*, Princeton, NJ: Princeton University Press.

Nasr, Seyyed Hossein (1993), *An Introduction to Islamic Cosmological Doctrines*, revised edn, Albany, NY: State University of New York Press.

Pines, Shlomo (1997), *Studies in Islamic Atomism*, translated by Michael Schwarz, Jerusalem: Magnes Press.

Preus, J. Samuel (2001), *Spinoza and the Irrelevance of Biblical Authority*, Cambridge: Cambridge University Press.

Rauschenbach, Sina (2002), *Josef Albo: Jüdische Philosophie und christliche Kontroverstheollogie in der frühen Neuzeit*, Leiden: Brill.

Reines, Alvin Jay (1970), *Maimonides and Abravanel on Prophecy*, Cincinnati, OH: Hebrew Union College Press.

Rudavsky, Tamar M. (2000), *Time Matters: Time, Creation, and Cosmology in Medieval Jewish Philosophy*, Albany, NY: State University of New York Press.

Samuelson, Norbert M. (1989), *An Introduction to Modern Jewish Philosophy*, Albany, NY: State University of New York Press.

Samuelson, Norbert M. (1994), *Judaism and the Doctrine of Creation*, Cambridge: Cambridge University Press.

Samuelson, Norbert M. (2002), *Revelation and the God of Israel*, Cambridge: Cambridge University Press.

Scholem, Gershom G. (1974), *Major Trends in Jewish Mysticism*, New York: Schocken.

Seeskin, Kenneth (1990), *Jewish Philosophy in a Secular Age*, Albany, NY: State University of New York Press.

Seeskin, Kenneth (2000), *Searching for a Distant God: The Legacy of Maimonides*, Oxford: Oxford University Press.

Seeskin, Kenneth (2001), *Autonomy in Jewish Philosophy*, Cambridge: Cambridge University Press

Silver, Daniel J. (1965), *Maimonidean Criticism and Maimonidean Controversy, 1180–1240*, Leiden: Brill.

Sirat, Colette (1985), *A History of Jewish Philosophy in the Middle Ages*, Cambridge: Cambridge University Press.

Smith, Steven B. (1997), *Spinoza, Liberalism, and the Question of Jewish Identity*, New Haven, CT: Yale University Press.

Smith, Steven B. (2003), *Spinoza's Book of Life: Freedom and Redemption in the Ethics*, New Haven, CT: Yale University Press.

Sorkin, David (1996), *Moses Mendelssohn and the Religious Enlightenment*, Berkeley, CA: University of California Press.

Tanenbaum, Adena (2002), *The Contemplative Soul: Hebrew Poetry and Philosophical Theory in Medieval Spain*, Leiden: Brill.

Tirosh-Rothschild, Hava (1991), *Between Worlds: The Life and Thought of Rabbi David ben Judah Messer Leon*, Albany, NY: State University of New York Press.

Tirosh-Samuelson, Hava (2003), *Happiness in Premodern Judaism: Virtue, Knowledge, and Well-Being*, Cincinnati, OH: Hebrew Union College Press.

Twersky, Isadore (1980), *Introduction to the Code of Maimonides (Mishneh Torah)*, New Haven, CT: Yale University Press.

Winston, David (1985), *Logos and Mystical Theology in Philo of Alexandria*, Cincinnati, OH: Hebrew Union College Press.

Wolfson, Elliot R. (1994), *Through a Speculum That Shines: Vision and Imagination in Medieval Jewish Mysticism*, Princeton, NJ: Princeton University Press.

Wolfson, Harry Austryn (1934 [1983]), *The Philosophy of Spinoza: Unfolding the Latent Processes of His Reasoning*, Cambridge, MA: Harvard University Press.

Wolfson, Harry Austryn (1957 [1971]), *Crescas' Critique of Aristotle: Problems of Aristotle's Physics in Jewish and Arabic Philosophy*, Cambridge, MA: Harvard University Press.

Wolfson, Harry Austryn (1975), *Philo: Foundations of Religious Philosophy in Judaism, Christianity, and Islam*, Cambridge, MA: Harvard University Press.

Wolfson, Harry Austryn (1979), *Repercussions of the Kalam in Jewish Philosophy*, Cambridge, MA: Harvard University Press.